the dead son

the dead son

david b. schock

PENULTIMATE · LTD

Copyright © 2022 David B. Schock

Published by penULTIMATE, Ltd.
545 Gidley Circle
Grand Haven, MI 49417

All rights reserved.

ISBN: 978-0-98941-014-4

Cover designed by Benjamin T. Lambright; school photo provided by David B. Schock.
Book edited, typeset, and designed by Amee Schmidt.

Dedication

This book is dedicated to Kathryn Mary "Katie Mairi" Neville, B.S., J.D., M.Div. It was her dedication to the wellbeing of children that attracted me—chief among her many other attributes. Her willingness to marry a widower, to move into the possibility of adopting three children ALL AT ONCE, and her strength and knowledge to negotiate the legal and social welfare system, made possible our extending a home to three precious children. She was their advocate in every sense of the word. And mine. She has been a loving partner to whom I am endlessly grateful.

Introduction

If you are reading this as a book it's because a lot of things had to happen. And they had to happen in a right way. My wife, Kathy, had not been able to read this in more than three years. It was too painful, too raw. Still, she gave her consent. There is so much that is intimately revealing of our family life, maybe too much. And then there is the possibility that the story still could harm our surviving children. This is a lot of their business that I'm putting out on the street. So, they have had a voice, too. They also agreed to its publication. My sense is that they lived this story, and they know many parts of it better than I. Kathy, too, has said that she remembers some things differently. When she started reading the book, she picked up a pencil to correct those remembrances. And then she put it down. This was, she realized, my telling of the story, not hers.

And an early reader took me to task, too, for what she called not finishing the book. She put it this way: "This is a 'Why God?' story that demands an answer. Your readers are members of families who have experienced the loss of a son or daughter to violent death. What can you tell them?"

Whatever I have to say about that is unlikely to satisfy. I cannot meet the demand. But this I can say: at the center of this story is, I believe, a God who is intimately concerned with our lives, our journey to Him.

I believe God was with David through his entire life, in his joy and loves, his suffering, his drunkenness, in his Methadone haze as he lay dying. . . . At his death. And beyond.

And I believe He is with our surviving children—JungYi and Daniel. And with Kathy and me. Even in days that are very dark, and there are many.

For those who demand a clear proof, I have nothing. By faith alone can I imperfectly comprehend this. It seems too much to take in. And yet the way forward is the way. That is the way of faith.

N.B. There will be passages from psychological assessments and from court records that may well seem too much for easy reading. I have long maintained that the art of reading is to skip judiciously. Skip as you like. Those records are included because courts and social workers have languages of their own. To the initiate, they tell a story. So, I leave them at length.

Saturday, July 13, 2013

Our son David came home today. Kathy was at the door to greet him, tears running down both cheeks. I pulled in the drive a few minutes later, but I'd had a good sense that he had arrived; the postman was completing his deliveries just down the street. I knew he had made a personal delivery. Kathy was still crying when I walked in from the garage.

Eight-pounds, five-point-two ounces, about the delivery weight of a healthy newborn. But the hand-written notice of content across the top of the box in felt-tip pen reveals other contents: "Contains human remains." I had warned our postman that this delivery was imminent just two days ago; we were expecting this.

It cost only thirty-five dollars and sixty cents to send our son by next-day delivery from the crematory in Mt. Prospect—on the north side of Chicago—to Grand Haven.

And now the box holding his cremains is sitting innocuously on the dining table.

Our son was 28 years old; we are grateful he made it that far. And we are ripped apart that this was how he came home. And that's enough.

Wednesday, July 3, 2013

I just settled in to watch a PBS special on the intelligence of dogs. Our little black mutt, some cross among and between a cattle dog, a pharaoh hound, maybe a lab and something else (or lots of somethings else) is watching, too. She sees the dogs on the wide-screen television and, thinking it a window to outside, goes tearing to the front door to look out on the street . . . sure that the dogs must be visible there, too. She makes the third trip, looking to me for some confirmation that her eyes are not deceiving her. I, of course, am laughing. Kathy is downstairs in our Grand Haven, MI, home.

My phone rings with a number I don't recognize. I answer and think at first it is our son David in turmoil, crying, trying to get words out. The meaning comes, haltingly, and it is our son Daniel calling, not David; their voices could be close at times.

> Dad . . . I have some really bad news. Your son, David, is dead. I came here after work, and I found him. This girl called me at work at 4:30 and said he wasn't responding. I told them to call an ambulance, and they didn't do it, and when I got here, he was dead, he was cold. Then the EMS was here. And they're in with him now, but he's dead. If only I'd gotten here sooner, but I couldn't leave work . . . .

I want to know where he is, where David is, what happened. Daniel is outside the house, and the EMS paramedics are inside. Daniel tells me he is waiting for them to bring out David's body. He doesn't mention being interviewed by the police, but perhaps that is yet to come.

David had been in and out of the hospital . . . the psych ward, and rehab for his alcoholism. He was depressed, homeless, unemployed and perhaps unemployable. He had been drinking. His new girlfriend, Jennifer, was a real piece of work, says Daniel, and she encouraged him to check himself out of the hospital where both of them had been patients and then moved in to her house where, Daniel says, she wanted him to impregnate her so that she could have a child to replace one who had died. And there were all these drugs there. There is more of his disdain of Jennifer, his assertion that her father is a police officer, that Jennifer is two weeks' pregnant with David's child, and how he blames himself for David's death. There is a lot of emotional content mixed up with what may be information.

I assure Daniel that I didn't think it his fault that his brother had died. This had been a possibility for a long, long time. Kathy and I knew that his trauma as a young man had left deep, and what seemed permanent, scars. Of our three children—our daughter and two sons—David was the most at risk.

I do not know if any of what Daniel had said was true. I know nothing about Jennifer.

And now this. Daniel says it is awful. He doesn't want to see David's body again. No, please. He'll never forget what he's seen.

I need to know more. I figure that David will have been transported to a local hospital. I research on the Internet what I thought were the closest medical centers in the Northwest Chicago area. I call Northwest Community Hospital where an attendant, Sean, tells me that David is not there. He suggests I might try St. Alexis Medical Center or Alexian Brothers Medical Center. He supplies the telephone numbers for both. I call the first and reach a woman—her name is not in my notes (why not?)—who was compassion itself. She lets me know David is not there, but I should hold the line. On her own she called the Cook County Medical Examiner's office and made inquiry. When she comes back on the line, she has information for me:

- David's body is still at the home.
- The address is 1145 North Belmont, Arlington Heights, IL 60004.
- Police are still at the scene investigating.
- Cook County Medical Examiner Johnson (Badge Number 73) is there and will take charge of the body (although not transport it).
- The case number is #042 July 2013.
- Stephen J. Cina, M.D., is the Chief Medical Examiner. (I write it down incorrectly as Dr. Zita, not the only mistake I'll make as I take notes.)

I am so grateful. I look up and call the Cook County Medical Examiner's Office. Investigator Santero tells me that the postmortem should be completed after 12:30 tomorrow, July 4. The holiday would make for a disrupted schedule. I ask and am told that I or we would not be able to view the body there. It was simply not possible. That means a mortuary service will be required. When I ask for a recommendation, I am told they can't give me one. But David's body would be held there cold for 30 days.

On his Facebook page Daniel posts an impromptu gathering:

> having a memorial for my brother aka Chino Dollaa tom july 4th around 10 pm. got 5 hundred dollars worth of fireworks to light off in his memory cuz that was one of his fav holidays . . . whoever was close to him and wants to join and pay respects is welcome . . . hit me up for info (224) -----------.

Thursday, July 4, 2013

Our desire is a direct cremation . . . no embalming. Basic, simple. It's what we do in our family. That would seem to preclude a funeral service with the body there . . . . Maybe with cremains, but any gathering will have to be the weekend after the Fourth. Through Kathy's niece, a mortician in Canada, we learn of a service called Basic Funerals. Basic. Yes, but with a good reputation. She gives us a number and I call and reach Eric Ferry. The body will likely be released on Monday, July 8th, but the holiday and following weekend will play havoc with schedules. Mr. Ferry has some domestic duties to attend to—time with a daughter—but he says he will begin working on this. In the meantime, there are lots of forms that needed filling out on the website. Could I start on those? Yes. Oh, and he thinks the cremation could take place on Tuesday at the nearby Monarch Cremation Society (part of the Sax-Tiedemann Funeral Home and Crematorium) in Franklin Park. At this stage we plan NOT to go to Chicago. I don't need to see my son's body to know that he is dead.

Friday, July 5, 2013

But our daughter, JungYi, does. She lives in southern California with her husband and daughter.[1] She wants to see David and to see us. She knows that seeing her brother for the last time also would involve seeing and staying with her biological mother. That will be difficult, but she will have to do it. JungYi's desire to see David's body will require a change in plans to allow for a short viewing. I know I'll have to call Mr. Ferry. But, assuming we can work out something, we volunteer a plane ticket for her, and she makes plans.

Saturday, July 6, 2013

Yes, we can get a full hour of visitation for only a little more money. That way JungYi can say goodbye to her brother. I tell Kathy that I will fly or drive over to be there. At first she doesn't see herself making the trip, but as I investigate, she realizes this will be important. She is not callous. David's death has leveled her, both of us, really. His death, while unwelcome, is not unexpected.

Two weeks previously he called me from a psych ward. He had been drinking and was despondent. He wanted it all to end. I begged him not to kill himself. I couldn't promise that things would get better immediately, but while there was life there was hope. All he needed was one opportunity. And then I said: "If you kill yourself, I will miss you like crazy."

---

[1] In 2014 they welcomed a son, too.

I would learn just how much.

I decide to fly. From O'Hare airport it's just a short cab ride to the funeral home/crematorium. Kathy told me to book for both of us. I am grateful not to have to do this by myself.

And suddenly things begin to spin out of control. Daniel now wants to see his brother, wants, in fact, to have an open house for all of David's friends. He says they NEED to see him, as does his biological mother, a former prostitute and drug dealer who lost custody of her children decades before (but who had re-inserted herself in her children's lives. The boys were living in Chicago because she promised them free money). There should be a full-blown funeral, says Daniel.

No, no, no, no. As far as their mother, she tore up her parent card a long time before. I understand she is grieving, but we do not want to see her, to come face to face with this woman. We have worked hard to keep her out of our lives.

Daniel calls back. He'll buy more time, he said. I explain to him that there will be no funeral and that it would be a bad idea to extend the time overmuch. When we arrive, David will still be cold from the cooler. It's a bad idea to leave a body, already five-days dead, at room temperature. Bad things start to happen, like skin-slip, gloving, and it can happen quickly. (I had experience living and working in a funeral home when I as a college sophomore. More about that presently.) Daniel is adamant. He'll pay for it. I give him Mr. Ferry's number. We hang up.

Daniel's girlfriend at the time, Monique, calls back and shouts at me: "If you were a Christian . . ." That's as far as she gets before I hang up.

Monique has tried to insinuate herself in this process earlier . . . telling Daniel what to say to me. I responded by telling Daniel this is not her business.

I call Mr. Ferry to warn him that things are devolving. He says he's seen these kinds of situations before and is glad to know before he gets the call from Daniel.

Daniel calls back and apologizes for Monique's behavior. She's had too much to drink, he says. She's upset. I'll understand when I meet her. I tell him I don't want to meet her, certainly not now. Nor do I want to meet the friends who suddenly think there will be a funeral party.

Sunday, July 7, 2013

Daniel again insists he's going to pay for extra time. Mr. Ferry gives him a number that stuns him: $500. No, he doesn't have that, can't raise it. But, says Daniel, I need to open the gathering. So many of David's friends are planning on coming. These are running buddies, some who are members of the Latin Kings.

My accommodation is this: Mr. Ferry will give us 15 more minutes. Kathy, JungYi, Daniel, and I, along with David's former girlfriend and her mother will claim the first 45 minutes. We want no one else there. After 45 minutes we'll leave and others—at the discretion of Mr. Ferry—will be allowed to see David's body. I warn Mr. Ferry that it's likely to grow ugly. He's seen a lot, he assures me; the police are already on his quick dial.

David's former long-term girlfriend, Maggie, had stuck by him through so much, even his incarceration for four years after he robbed a bank. After his release from prison David had lived for several years with her and her mother. But of late, his drinking claimed him so strongly there was nothing left over. He was given to verbal abuse and even violence when intoxicated. And when he was drunk, he wanted to stay drunk; he'd work at it.

She needed him to get sober, something only he could do for himself. So, they broke up, and he had to go out on his own. I give her a lot of credit. She developed a boundary to protect herself.

This amazing Maggie and her mother volunteer to come and gather us at the O'Hare Airport. We gratefully accept. We know and cherish her from phone conversations and even a visit with David at our home. We explain to her what we know that is transpiring with Daniel (which is not the half of it).

Monday, July 8, 2013

We learn that Daniel has been contacting members of his biological family, telling them that he has to bury his brother, and he needs their financial help. He's been saying that it's all on him.

Tuesday, July 9, 2013

Kathy and I fly directly from Muskegon to O'Hare. We are booked on the return flight four hours after we arrive. Maggie and her mother collect us. We stop for a chance to talk and eat at the nearby restaurant. This is a grim gathering and the last chance for calm.

We arrive at the funeral home, go immediately to the wrong door, the door leading to the attached residence. We regain the pathway, find the front door, enter and meet Mr. Ferry. We have tried to keep him in the loop of everything that's been going on. He sympathizes, knowing families can be messy. Our daughter is already there. Kathy and I hug her fiercely. Daniel arrives and reaches to embrace me. I do not respond quickly, and he senses it. A young woman who I gather to be Monique hovers in the background. I look at her directly—probably glare at her—and she steps back. Mr. Ferry joins us.

I do not want to go see my dead son.

I want to go see my dead son.

Mr. Ferry precedes us and opens the double doors to a rather shabby parlor. At the head of the room is a cardboard box, a cremation casket. I follow immediately behind Mr. Ferry and see my son's hawkish profile. Even in death he is elegant, beautiful. I feel like I'm leading a tour: to Kathy—here is our son, to JungYi and Daniel—here is your brother, to Maggie—here is your heart's true love . . . . I stand, I look, I touch his hands, his face. Yes, cold. That's good. We had not asked for any cosmetic services, but I think there is a trace of blush on his cheek, his eyes are firmly closed and not slackly open. It all seems incongruous.

David was tall, thin, well-muscled. If he wasn't dead, he would have been striking. He and his siblings were very attractive/handsome/beautiful: half Korean and the other half Cherokee, Irish, and Scots (I always joked that you had to look out for that Scots . . . which pretty well describes Kathy . . . a Staffin Lassie whose family came from the east coast of Skye).

I see the cranial autopsy sutures across the top of his head, clearly visible in his short-cropped hair. I think Mr. Ferry tried to darken them to allow them to not stand out quite so much.

All of us stand at the casket and just look. Daniel says some things . . . that he blames himself. He says how when we'd send David some small sum they would buy alcohol and sit in a car drinking. He again tells the story of coming right from work after telling Jessica to call the EMTs. There are variations. I tell him that I do not believe that David's death is his fault. I do not think it is. Now or later.

Time carries on. Maggie, David's former girlfriend, wants a few minutes by herself with his body. I don't have to understand in order to acquiesce.

We didn't contact any clergy in the area; after all, there was to be no funeral. But our retired parish priest equipped me with a small bottle of anointing oil, and I had consulted the Book of Common Prayer, our prayer book in the Anglican Church.

And so I stand again and for the last time at his side and read from a sheet I had printed out, The Commendation intended for a blessing after death. There are plenty of other prayers for the times before and at death.

A Commendatory Prayer when the Soul is Departed.

INTO thy hands, O merciful Saviour, we commend the soul of thy servant, now departed from the body. Acknowledge, we humbly beseech thee, a sheep of thine own fold, a lamb of thine own flock, a sinner of thine own redeeming. Receive *him* into the arms of thy mercy, into the blessed rest of everlasting peace, and into the glorious company of the saints in light. *Amen*.

I take the cap off the bottle and tilt it to wet my thumb with oil and proceed to

The Anointing

I anoint thee with oil, In the Name of the Father, and of the Son, and of the Holy Ghost.

Then comes

The Committal

**He who raised Jesus Christ from the dead
will also give new life to our mortal bodies
through his indwelling Spirit.**

**My heart, therefore, is glad, and my spirit rejoices;
my body also shall rest in hope.**

**You will show me the path of life;
in your presence there is fullness of joy,
and in your right hand are pleasures for evermore.**

**In sure and certain hope of the resurrection to eternal life
through our Lord Jesus Christ, we commend to Almighty
God our brother, David, and we commit *his* body to be burnt;
earth to earth, ashes to ashes, dust to dust. The Lord bless
him and keep *him*, the Lord make his face to shine upon *him*
and be gracious to *him*, the Lord lift up his countenance upon
him and give *him* peace. *Amen*.**

The penultimate utterance is

The Lord's Prayer

**Our Father, who art in heaven,
  hallowed be thy Name,
  thy kingdom come,
  thy will be done,
    on earth as it is in heaven.
Give us this day our daily bread.
And forgive us our trespasses,
  as we forgive those
    who trespass against us.
And lead us not into temptation,
  but deliver us from evil.
For thine is the kingdom,
  and the power, and the glory,
  for ever and ever. Amen.**

And, lastly:

Rest eternal grant to *him*, O Lord;
***And let light perpetual shine upon* him.**

**May his soul, and the souls of all the departed,
through the mercy of God, rest in peace.** *Amen.*

It is time to surrender our dead son to his living brother, their biological mother, and whoever else is here. We exit the parlor. Those who were waiting to come in step back. We see them, including a couple who had taken care of the boys when they first came to us, all those years ago. Daniel must have called them.

Maggie and her mother return us to the airport, and we come home.

Friday, July 12, 2013

I call the Arlington Heights Police Department to see if I can get more information, and I am told by Kellie Lichtenberger that I will need to file a FOIA—a Freedom of Information Act request—to get it. I also need to show some identification. I scan my driver's license and send it via the Internet along with the filled-out request to the records supervisor and FOIA manager, Maureen Schmidt. Here's what I write to her:

> Dear Maureen Schmidt:
>
> I understand from Kelly that you are the FOIA coordinator. I am seeking information about my son's death July 3, 2013. I understand as well that the investigation may not be concluded. I do not mind waiting until it is . . . if that cuts you any slack.
>
> I have a call in to Det. William Kirby; I understand he is in charge of the case.
>
> And if there is any fee for the records, please let me know.
>
> I thank you for taking the time to deal with this. I am so grateful.
>
> Sincerely,

There is a space on the FOIA form to indicate what it is I am after. This is what I write:

> Anything to do with my son's death. My son was David Herbert McNutt Schock, DOD July 3, 2013, at 1145 North Belmont, Arlington Heights, IL. Case number 13-11812, Det. William Kirby.

The request is fulfilled the next day, the same day our son comes home. Mrs. Schmidt indicates that the request is granted in part and denied in part . . . but the only denial is on the three-page police report: the contact information for the person who reported David's death. Fair enough.

There is lots and lots of information there for me to consider. There is, for instance, the narrative of the lead responding officer, Thomas Croon:

> In summary, on 7-3-13 we were dispatched to 1145 N. Belmont reference an ambulance call later reclassified a sudden death. We arrived on scene along with Arlington Heights Paramedics Eschner #215, Forde #210, Rodgers #137, Simon #158, Moran #173 and Harris #187. Upon entry to the residence victim David Schock was laying on his back on the living room floor just outside the entrance to the kitchen. David was wearing a white t-shirt and blue pants. Paramedics immediately began life saving efforts. After numerous attempts their life saving efforts proved unsuccessful and David was pronounced dead at 1959 hours by Northwest Community Hospital Dr. Silver. AHFD's run number was 4955.
>
> Jennifer Stoeckel is the girlfriend of victim David Schock. She was on scene along with her mother Kathleen Stoeckel and the victim's brother Daniel Schock. While paramedics were working on David we spoke with the other parties on scene.
>
> Jennifer advised she believes David ingested methadone Zanex (sic.) and alcohol sometimes in the morning. At approximately 1230 hours David told her he did not feel good and fell down in the living room but did not loose (sic) consciousness. Jennifer advised David remained in a lethargic state until approximately 1630 hours. At 1630 hours she advised she put him in a living room chair for him to sleep. Jennifer stated David was breathing until approximately 1915 hours when her mother Kathleen noticed he was not breathing and called 911. Jennifer and her mother moved David from the chair to the living room floor to begin CPR until AHFD arrived.
>
> Commander Kearney #627, Sgt. Boggs #5540, Detective Sgt Kappelman #530, Detective Commers #309 and Detective Kirby #295 arrived on scene to assist with the investigation. Jennifer Stoeckel and Daniel Schock were transported to AHPD for further investigation.
>
> Forensic Technicians Ruge #274 and Felser #249 were on scene and processed the scene per department directive. See FT Ruge's report for further.
>
> David's mother, Huicha McNutt, was advised of the death by her son and David's brother, Daniel Schock.
>
> At 2042 hours I contacted the Cook County Medical Examiner's office and spoke with investigator Johnson #73. After hearing the facts of the case he requested the victim be transported to the medical examiners (sic) office and assigned to the victim case number 042July13. At approximately 2145 hours official from Lauterberg & Oehler arrived on scene and transported the victim to the medical examiner office without incident. NFA.

Officer Croon typed up his report and filed it at 21:26 of July 3. His report was reviewed by watch commander Thomas Boggs at 22:30.

Additional information indicated that the call came in at 19:15 and that the emergency forces arrived at 19:17. Two minutes. That's fast response. And what a response: seven EMS paramedics, the commander, a sergeant, a detective sergeant, and two detectives. No shortage of help, and ranking help at that.

Kathy notes that such firepower seems unusual. There may be a reason. Jennifer's father, Alan Stoeckel, was at the time, the deputy Chief of Field Operations for the Palatine Police Department.[2]

It truly is too soon to judge exactly what happened, but if the accounts of the events from Jennifer Stoeckel and our son Daniel are correct, our son ingested a lethal dose of drugs and perhaps alcohol and his "girlfriend" put him in a chair and let him die without summoning aid. Would she have known that his death would eventuate? And where was Daniel in all this? I only know what he told me when he called to tell me of David's death on the evening of July 3.

I twice try to reach Detective William Kirby, the investigator. My thought is he may have been laboring under the misapprehension that David's biological mother is his next of kin. She is not; we are. I leave a message.

In her cover memo, Mrs. Schmidt suggests that I file another request for additional information in six weeks or so when the investigation is complete.

Monday, July 15, 2013

I call in the morning and am told that Detective Kirby will be available in the afternoon. He is. He says he had known David in the old days when he had been running with the Latin Kings. He'd had to deal with him a few times. He did not know about the bank robbery and resulting incarceration, he says, just that he hadn't seen David in a long while. He is pleasant, as helpful as he can be, and he understands what parents go through. He sorrowed in David's death. He is perhaps not altogether surprised; people who lead rough lives often die young.

And all the officers at the scene? That would not be unusual even if the home had not belonged to someone in law enforcement. "That's the normal number. Any unresponsive person is going to get that response."

As for Daniel's involvement, Detective Kirby says when he first saw Daniel, he was busy trying to hide or discard marijuana and drug bottles with David's name on them.

---

[2] In 2014 he ascended to the position as Chief of Police. As such he supervised 109 officers. Ho, Sally. "New top cop named in Palatine," *Chicago Tribune*, March 7, 2014. https://www.chicagotribune.com/suburbs/ct-xpm-2014-03-07-ct-new-police-chief-palatine-tl-nw-20140307-story.html He retired in 2019.

As far as Jennifer's recounting what exactly happened: "That's a bullshit story."

But he says there are no charges pending: "It would be damned near impossible to get a charge with this for a drug-induced murder," he said. For that, prosecutors would have to be able to prove that someone—presumably Jennifer—had intended for David to take her Methadone. And there were no grounds to consider criminal facilitation. Depraved indifference? Probably not. There was nothing there to charge anyone with anything in David's taking of the fatal dose.

If we want to, we can try a civil suit, he says. We have no interest. None.

Tuesday, January 3, 2017

This is a mighty time jump, but we'll be going forward and backward. I will do my best to signpost time shifts.

The mail has at long last brought a package from the Cook County Medical Examiner's Office . . . not through any fault of the Examiner's office; I had delayed sending in the money to pay for the materials. Maybe a six-month delay. Do I really want it?

I find the mailer on the dining room table—where most of our mail gets dropped when it's brought in from the curbside mailbox. Kathy certainly knew what it was when she placed it there. I told her I was in communication with the Medical Examiner's office, starting in July of last year, to get everything possible about David's death . . . all the reports, all the conclusions, all the images. I can feel that it's been shipped on a disk, whatever it is. As long as the envelope is not open, I don't have to remember what's there, and I will not see and re-see the images of his body minus the animating force. I expect the photos will show the postmortem as it goes along. For now, he remains whole in my thoughts. But I know better.

Saturday, January 7, 2017

Calvarium. That's the word that rings in my brain, the word I whisper to myself.

No, I have not yet opened the envelope . . . but I know I will soon. And that word will be there.

So now I'm chattering. I whistle in the dark when I'm afraid.

The calvarium is the top part of the skull, the dome, the cranial vault.

Calvarium . . . Calvary. Or, in Koinē Greek, Golgatha. It translates to "the place of the skull," a hill that resembles a skullcap, a Calvarium. It's where Jesus and the two others were crucified. Oh, and probably thousands of others before and after.

Calvarium. In a postmortem, a part of it is sawn with an oscillating bone saw—probably a Stryker 810—to take it off. Really, it's much like carving a pumpkin, but with a high-tech tool. It has to be wielded very carefully in order to preserve the underlying meninges and the brain itself. If you do it right, you want to be sure the dissected bone will reset firmly and that there is a notch of some sort to lock it in place.

I know this because I have watched the procedure dozens of times. As a sophomore at Albion College, I lived and worked in a funeral home. There was no morgue at the city hospital, so the pathologist would pull up behind the mortuary in his little Mercedes 280 SL, and he'd call for help either from my roommate, George, or me. Which one of us would glove up depended on who didn't have a class. If neither one of us was available, one the funeral home owners would fill the bill.

My first postmortem was of a young girl who'd died as a result of a car accident. I recall the circumstances of her death: her mother was driving her to school, and there was a crash. The girl, a preteen, was not wearing a seatbelt and was thrown up and under the dash into the heater. Her autopsy was the first time I heard the whine of a bone saw . . . and that came after the pathologist made a scalp cut across the top of the head from side to side, retracted one flap forward across the face and the other backward toward the neck, in all exposing the calvarium. That sawing would take some time. These days, pathologists have negative pressure in the post rooms, and they wear face shields. Back then, the cloud and smell of hot bone hung in the white-tiled room. The pathologist was kind and knew of my interest in physiology and anatomy. He said he theorized that this girl died of a circumferential fracture at the base of the skull. He'd seen it many times before, and it was far more common than most people realized. With her cerebellum exposed he confirmed his supposition by running his index finger between the inside of the skull and the back of the brain. When he withdrew that finger, he asked me to do the same: "What happened is that her skull fractured all along the base, and you can feel something like sand . . . those are tiny bone fragments." It did feel like grit. Some adhered to the glove when I withdrew my finger. I rolled it between my thumb and forefinger. At my question, he explained that she would likely have been unconscious upon impact and would have died within minutes. And there would have been nothing that could have saved her.

In addition to the girl's craniotomy, the pathologist that day cut into and explored the chest and abdominal cavities. Using a "Y"-shaped cut from each shoulder to the breastbone, and then down to the gut. He used bone cutters to snap the ribs. It's inelegant but effective. In particular, he was looking for something called chest flail . . . when the outside of the body stops moving suddenly but the inside rips apart as it keeps traveling for a little bit. That's how Princess Diana died.

He took out the lungs and heart, too. He inspected stomach contents. He wanted detailed answers in this unnatural death.

After everything was weighed and measured and very small samples were taken, it all went back more or less in place. One other thing I learned that day was the double-curve autopsy needle and the baseball stitch that he used to close the head and other wounds after the return of organs and structures.

The scalp suturing was very fine. "It normally will be unnoticeable because it will be covered by hair," he said. "But you want to make it look as inconspicuous as possible."

The "Y" incision that revealed the chest and abdomen was of a more rapid running seam with much heavier suture, but very neat as well.

And there were a dozen or more other autopsies after that. I never did faint, but there were a couple times when I didn't feel exactly my best. I think about all those times and the half dozen or so other times I've been to the local morgue at Butterworth Hospital in Grand Rapids to interview forensic pathologist Stephen Cohle for the films I have made about unsolved homicides—what I call delayed justice cases.

David's death is not a murder—perhaps the result of indifference, but not outright murder—but his is an unnatural death, so an autopsy is required; it will likely be very much like those I had stood through and assisted. Only now it is my loved one on the table, however briefly that might run, in Cook County. Maybe beginning and end times are listed. I'll just have to see.

For now, I've run out of chatter.

Later . . .

I more or less force myself into these situations. Inside the mailer is a CD with 12 images of my dead son. The reports are likely, then, to follow. I open the images in the small previewer, first to see if I can stand it.

And then I open them fully. In the first photograph, a close-up of his face, his eyes are halfway open, like he is barely paying attention to what is going on around him. What has all the commotion of the morgue to do with his passing into eternity? I have seen that look before, but this time there is no mistake that the life force has withdrawn. His lips are parted slightly to reveal his very white teeth, and the corners of his mouth remain slightly upturned, not as slack as I might expect. He does not look at ease, at rest; he looks distressed.

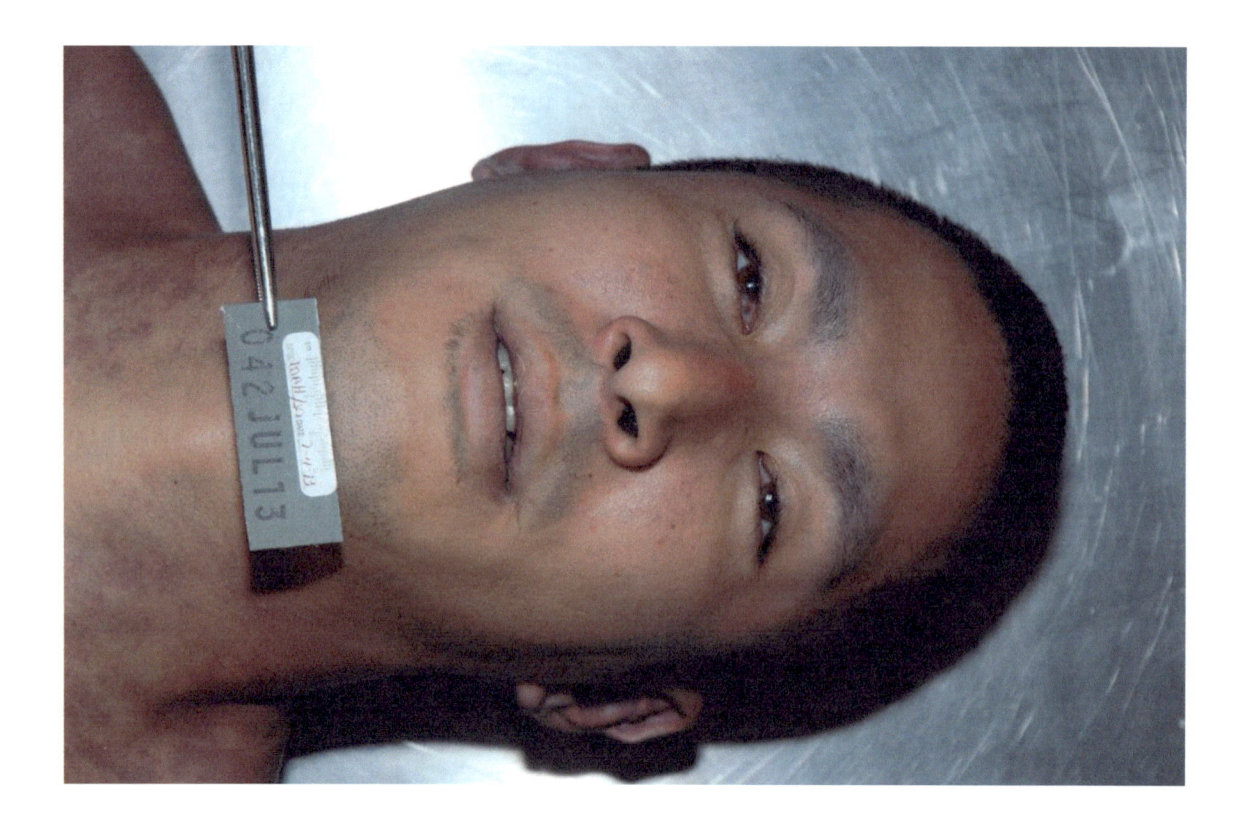

In other shots, I see revealed the electrodes they placed on his ankles to try to bring him back. He is thin but not emaciated. Not an ounce of fat, but there never was. There are several tattoos. I never understood how this little boy who hated needles could grow up to endure the process of tattooing. I knew about the one all across his shoulder blades that spelled out his last name in capital Old English lettering, SCHOCK. Kathy and I had seen that and studied it the last time David came home. At the time he was doing well, mostly sober, and he and Maggie drove from Chicago to Grand Haven for a day visit in the high heat of summer. David and I had posed for a picture, my tee shirt soaked through and rimed with sweat salt. I look hot (but happy), and he looks cool.

Later that day, we went downstairs to play some trumpet duets. I have spent most of my life playing as a professional musician . . . at least part-time. And as a boy, he wanted to play, so I bought him a really good trumpet, and he kept at it for a time, at least until things got out of hand and he started into drugs. When he came home, he wanted to try to play again, so we descended to my office. It was hot enough even down there—and he was working hard enough that he was overheated—so he peeled off his shirt. There was the tattoo. Impressive by any standards. So, we had seen that tattoo.

And there is a shot of it, the black letters against the liver-colored pooled blood on his upper back.

But the other tattoo that is photographed is a surprise. It must be newer; it wasn't there at our last visit.

I understand it as soon as I see it. Or, I think I do.

A lion. On his left breast. It makes its own perfect sense.

The other pictures reveal David previous to the autopsy. It is a relief that I don't have to see him pieced out. As for the autopsy report . . . I'll have to read it when it arrives later.

How did we get here?

JungYi, David, and Daniel came to us. That's the language we use, but the reality is this: we went to Florida and brought them back to live with us in Michigan. They were 13, 9, and 8. The year was 1995 and Kathy and I had been married for three years.

Prior to our marriage I had been married with her best friend since eighth grade, Barbara Jo Stephenson. Jo and I had been married May 20, 1972, and stayed very married until her death of adenocarcinoma on July 8, 1991.

When Kathy and I married June 27, 1992, there was a question of whether there would be children. It might have been physically possible, but the odds were against it, and the risks of a late-in-life pregnancy were considerable for Kathy and any child. So, we began talking about adoption, even before we were married.

Kathy had taken the step of subscribing to a monthly list of available adoptees, half-sheets each with a photo and details. These were mostly older children. I think her reasoning was that if we were considering adoption options, we needed to consider all kinds of things: origin, race, circumstances, illnesses or congenital conditions. Kathy told me that there wasn't much that would rule out a child. For example, children with Down's syndrome often were the joy of families and their lives were precious. (Kathy had previously been a caseworker with an area agency; she was well familiar with people of differing abilities.) I had thought perhaps of children who were left orphaned because of parents who had died of AIDS. I wasn't sure of a transracial adoption in predominantly white Grand Haven.

One of the things the availability sheets did was to open the idea of adopting siblings; surely these were the hardest to place and the most in need.

One day Kathy came home from a trip to Lansing where she was working, and she said she had a message through the car radio. It was this: "You need to get a home study done at once." No, it wasn't an ad or something that was part of a program. She understood it was God speaking.

A home study is the first step in the adoptive process. An independent evaluator talks with the prospective adoptive parents, makes several home visits, investigates financial soundness, emotional health, the likelihood that a couple will stay together through the strains of taking on a child to love and raise.

The man who did that work was Dick Van Deelen of Adoption Associates. Dick told us some of his story. At one point he had worked for Bethany Services, a large, Christian agency. By the time we were considering adopting, he was part of a loose association of adoption professionals. In other words, he had a wide network of friends and associates.

And he was pretty blunt about it all: white babies, blond- and blue-eyed, cost this much. Russian babies cost this much; Chinese babies, Korean babies, Ethiopian babies, this much. There were some limitations on adopting Native American babies, something relatively new, and there might be issues with adopting Black American babies.

It was at that meeting, fairly late in the process, that Kathy spoke up.

"David and I were talking, and he doesn't think it's going to be a baby. In fact, he sees a sibling group . . . an older sister and two younger brothers."

As Kathy said, I had told her what I had seen in my mind—more than imagination. Perhaps that seeing had been informed by the adoption availability sheets, but I "saw" the three children as if they were standing before me.

Neither of us discounted the perception of the other; I paid attention when she said we needed the home study and, as she related what I had told her, she stated it as more or less fact. She trusted it; we'd already experienced too much in our life together to discount inklings that might be described as coming from outside ourselves.

But Dick was astounded.

"If these are older children, chances are that they will have been through the abuse and neglect system. They'll be wrecked. And three??? Are you sure you'd be up to the challenge?"

We didn't know.

"And it's likely that it will take a long time until such a sibling trio presents."

We told him there was no hurry.

At that I felt a little relief because the process had been moving pretty fast. So, we went home to wait and work. Kathy agreed that it was likely going to be a very long wait.

Until the next day.

Kathy took the call from Dick, and she said it went something like this: "I was so . . . impressed . . . with our conversation that I wanted to talk it over with one of my friends who is down in Florida. Mel and I had worked together at Bethany. I was telling him 'I have this qualified couple and the husband says he sees a sibling trio . . . an older sister and two younger brothers . . . and I've told them that it would be extremely unusual . . . .' That's as far as I got when Mel asked if I was sitting down. I said I was. And then he told me that just yesterday he had to disrupt a pre-adoptive placement of this sibling trio—an older sister and two younger brothers—who had come into his care. It was a really unusual case. Not through the traditional social services path. The mom was no place in the picture and the dad—an alcoholic drug abuser—had surrendered custody. And Mel doesn't know what he's going to do with them.

"So, there you are."

We were not surprised. There was to be no waiting.

The children were in Florida where they had been living with their father. So, we'd need to fly down to meet them.

My opinion remains unchanged: Florida is largely a muggy swamp.

I recall that we flew into the Ft. Lauderdale-Hollywood Airport, rented a car, and followed directions to a low-budget motel where we had reservations (more so after we saw the place). So much of that trip remains unremembered. I do recall meeting the three children at the house where two of them were staying. And the youngest, Daniel, had a foot and ankle in a cast; he'd gotten caught in a car door, dragged, and run over when the driver backed up. He was not easily persuaded to use the ill-fitting crutches that he'd been given to protect the fracture that had been encased in the cheapest possible plaster welfare cast.

We met each other. For their part, immediately out of what had been an abusive pre-adoptive placement, they were wary. We saw three exhausted children. The oldest, the sister, JungYi, had taken on the role of parent to David and Daniel . . . and herself. She was responsible. But so young for the job. Still, she'd been doing it for years.

We would learn about the children. Their education was at best spotty. They'd been moved so often, most recently with their father living in an abandoned gas station and retrieving food that had been discarded from stores. There had been plenty of homeless shelters, but their father's continuing alcohol use kept them out of many of them. And he was not prone to following rules.

Their mother had been a native of Seoul. She and their father had met when he was stationed in Korea. They married when she told him she was pregnant. If she had been, the pregnancy ended even before she accompanied him back to the States . . . Knoxville. In short order they had three children. He was drinking and had no job, and his family could only do so much to help them; she began prostituting herself and found an underground network of other Koreans. Facing the of yet another arrest, she vanished.

And their father took them to Florida. Along the way they observed him getting beaten nearly to death in a fight and watched him cavorting with teenage prostitutes—in short, they saw everything children should never see, much less experience. It was JungYi who nursed him after he'd been in a fight and clubbed repeatedly with a galvanized steel water pipe.

By the time they were nosed out by authorities in Florida, their father willingly signed over custody. He knew that he was not able to take care of them. And they knew it, too.

We took the children to an interactive museum and nature center, sort of to get to know each other in a public place. It may have been the next day that we went to an IMAX film, the first and only one I've ever seen.

And then there was a dinner at an Outback Steakhouse, but we were there with everybody . . . Mel and his wife, Marion, as well as the members of the two families that were housing the children.

At some point there was a business discussion with Mel. He was blunt: the children were not in a good situation, temporary at best, and if we had any interest, unlike most adoptions where it's good to take time, in this instance, it might be best to hurry things along.

The adoption fee would be $10,000 to his agency, Shepherd Care; Mel figured he had that much already invested in the children. I explained that we didn't have that much money on hand. Mel said we were good for it.

We talked about the failed pre-adoptive placement: the prospective parents turned out to have a lot of issues and were simply not equipped to dealing with these children in addition to their own biological child. On investigation, it had been a disaster; that's why Mel took the measure of abruptly disrupting the placement.

In a normal situation, the children would have had months to process the idea of another pre-adoptive placement; they'd have talked with counselors, and there would have been many meetings with us. They'd have had a chance to say what they wanted and how they felt about it all.

But this was not a normal situation. There was no long-term placement plan other than with us.

Deep end of the pool for them and for us.

Sunday, January 15, 2017

Today is David's 32nd birthday.

So much of what's gone before in this account has been chewing at me. So much of what's yet to come is going to do more. It deals with being an imperfect parent in what seemed (but wasn't) an impossible situation.

There in Florida we decided to adopt the three children. If we were going to adopt, this was the time and these were the children, even with all the challenges clearly present. We knew there would be others, many others.

I had to fly back before Kathy. I had a contract to fulfill with Dow Corning to produce some videos; I had shoots set up, and I had to be there. I signed whatever documents were required on my part in order to begin the adoptive process, and I left Kathy to sign the rest.

She was staying an extra three days and the matter of bringing the children north was left entirely on her.

When it came time to return, she had to negotiate Florida traffic with a car filled with three apprehensive children and then endure three plane changes, distant gates, and delayed flights. Daniel, because of his broken foot and thick cast, had to be wheeled in a chair or—more often—carried in her arms.

Though they were once more delayed, I was at the Gerald A. Ford Airport in Grand Rapids when they staggered off the plane at some middle-of-the-night hour. It took a little more than an hour to drive to our home in Grand Haven.

My first piece of advice for the children was to leave Archie—the cat—alone. If they chased him, he would hide and not come out for days, if ever.

The kids clambered into the house from the car, dropped what they were carrying and set off in swift search for Archie. For his part, Archie had come to our bedroom door—he had been napping there, looked about, yawned, and then saw the trio heading his way. He fled under the bed, and despite their efforts, the children didn't get to pet him for months. Finally, he assented when they began to settle a little.

A little horseplay at the front door. David had borrowed Daniel's crutch.

And that settling! The children were incapable of sitting at a table through a meal; they were up and about, moving here and there. We started on a shaky card table. One would want more milk, and would jump up to get it, another had to go to his bedroom and get something. Sometimes they would just wander away, taking food with them.

Little by little, they came to sit and talk while eating. We bought a large old cherry table that had come from a northern Michigan resort. It was an antique, I guess, but it was big and solid. The rush-bottomed seats gave them enough height that they could easily swing their legs. We started manners contests . . . what to do and why at the table, and elsewhere. How to behave in stores. How to behave at the YMCA. How to behave in a restaurant. That one was especially difficult.

Except for K-Garden. The legendary Grand Rapids Korean restaurant was nothing fancy, but for us it was a palace. We sought it out, thinking that the children had long missed their biological mother's cooking. They talked about it all the time. The store-bought kimchi recalled other tables and other meals. So, we wanted to make something nice happen for them.

The owners, husband and wife, offered real Korean food, but also billed the restaurant as a home for Chinese food. There were probably ten small tables. The first time we walked in, the wife looked at the kids, came over and spoke to them in Korean, grabbing their cheeks. They were incandescent. We were led to a table and all three began asking for food. David started crying. He wanted that one food, the one his mother used to make, and he didn't know what it was called.

The wife hugged him. "I make for you," she said. That was the extent of our ordering. And she was right. When she put a plate of bulgogi—marinated grilled beef—before them, they cried. And ate. And ate. All the delicacies of their first childhood were there before them.

We would come again and again to K-Garden. It was a spiritual feeding, said Kathy.

It would be fair to say we were overwhelmed. And the needs for their care could be unrelenting.

We needed help, and needed it immediately. In the first place, Kathy and I were scheduled, and had been for a year, to travel to Greece with my late wife's parents. This was both a family event and a reward for editing a book for my father-in-law. We WOULD be making the trip. We lined up Kathy's mother, Mairi, and Andrea, the daughter of a dear friend and mentor. Everything was in place, even though the children had known us for less than a month, and we were off. Oh, we felt the tug before, during and after, but we both wanted and were committed to go.

And who could be a better caretaker than Kathy's mother? She had spent years with other grandchildren; she even spent time volunteering to cuddle newborns in the neonatal unit at her hospital in Windsor. She enjoyed and loved children of all ages. And she loved ours without reservation. And Andrea was close to JungYi's age and could have a real impact. Both of them worked diligently while we were gone.

I don't know if others will find fault for our taking the trip, but we did it and the outcome was everything we could have hoped for. Yes, there were regular and frequent calls home, but there was nothing going on there that could have been classified as an emergency. (And as a good attorney, Kathy had prepared all the legal documents necessary to see that her mother could make any decision necessary.)

We came home rested and eager for what was ahead. But still there was the need for additional help with the kids that first fall.

After several unsuccessful tries, we found a daycare provider that late summer who would take on the boys during the days. Soon I was off teaching pretty much all day long at nearby Hope College, and Kathy worked as an independent contractor for the state. Her office was in the home. She needed order.

Laurie filled the bill admirably, at least at the start. She and her husband, Howie, really liked the boys and asked permission to take them all kinds of places. One time the couple took them to a trade show in Grand Rapids. The boys came back with pictures standing next to a scantily clad model. Hmmm. Once we learned that Howie had been driving well in excess of 100 miles per hour on a trip to the Mackinac Bridge, we said "No more" until Laurie assured us that she'd monitor the driving.

We had appreciated their help, and they and we had grown close. Certainly, our children loved them, especially the boys.

At one point, needing assurance for a future we hoped wouldn't happen, we asked them if in the event of our deaths, they'd take on the children as their own. (We had cause to rethink that later.) Howie was standing at one of our windows overlooking the bayou in the backyard and the scene up the river, and I asked his thought. "Yeah," he said, "this would be a nice place to live." It was unnerving. I would come to remember that.

At this point we had our hands full, and we tried to come up with creative solutions. We had started grammar contests. I think my favorite interrogatory from the children was "Why come?" I say it to myself often these days.

And their casual reference to "poop" was the distinctly Southern "dookie." Their language was alive and creative, but we wanted them to have a choice of speech, thinking ours was semi-standard.

And to help them, there would need to be school. But they had missed so much, been bounced through so many classrooms that there was no chance a regular public school would suit. And how would a public school sort all of their history? There was documentation; the children came with reams of paperwork.

And now, in looking over David's life, I have taken the closest look ever at his educational history.

The first record we have of David's education was from 1990 and 1991 in Jefferson County Public Schools, Louisville, KY.

As a first grader, he attended Croissant Park Elementary and Bennett Elementary, both in Ft. Lauderdale, Broward County. At Bennett his teacher had something nice to say:

> David is making good progress this term. He completes all work neatly and carefully. Encourage David to write short stories. He participates often in class. I've enjoyed working with David this year.

She promoted him.

And by the time he was in second grade, he, his sister, and his brother were already out of their father's voluntarily relinquished custody, living in foster care in Palm Beach County. David was attending Loxahatchee Groves Elementary. David had been singled out as behind in his reading and language skills and highly distractible. There was nothing he was doing that was malicious, but at times he could be somewhat disruptive at school and at home, too, according to the foster parent.

I imagine the world must have been a chaotic place. And there had been enough disruption that very little might seem stable.

In early December of 1993 his second-grade teacher wrote:

> David has difficulty staying on task. He plays with things in his desk constantly. He plays and talks when instruction is going on. When his attention is called he gets back on task for a while. David seems to be stronger in math. He is having difficulty in reading. His vocabulary is very weak. When he comes to a word he doesn't know he just stops. Very weak phonic skills.

In his birth family, only his father spoke English. Had they tested him for Korean comprehension, the testers might have been in for a surprise.

In a checklist she noted that he frequently read word-by-word, and always read below grade level. He frequently had difficulty closing words vocally, sometimes got mixed up on sound/symbol associations, often forgot what he read, always preferred to print, and could not tell time to the minute . . . all skills expected at that age.

In a separate note she wrote: "David has difficulty staying on task—or even in his seat."

He was referred for both assessment concerning the possibility of attention deficit hyperactivity disorder (ADHD) AND for removal of warts on his hands.

The classroom observer came into his class after the start of the new year. She studied David during a morning journal-writing activity. All the children—a room full of second graders—started the process on the floor.

9:30—Swinging arms/plays with shoes/raises hand/watching teacher/slaps legs/puts feet on chair in front of him/talks with neighbor/kneeling/sitting on legs/raises hand to respond to fix sentence errors

9:35—Watches as corrections are made/listening position appropriate/hand up/unties sneakers—fingers laces/watching students do corrections/talks to neighbor/hand up/hand up/swings arms

9:37—pulls, fingers laces/smiling/talking to neighbor/fingers laces/hand up/sitting appropriate/hand up "I Will"/smiling, listening/laces around ankle

9:39—Hand up/sitting/fingering laces/row 1 (David's row) instructed to return seat + begin journal writing

9:40—Sits/laces tied/stands, turns/ bends to go into desk/removes journal/sits/begins writing on task

9:41—On task/sitting approp./working on second sentence "Today s Friday January 14, 1994." "Toroe Timor is my birthday." "I am going on an airboat ride."

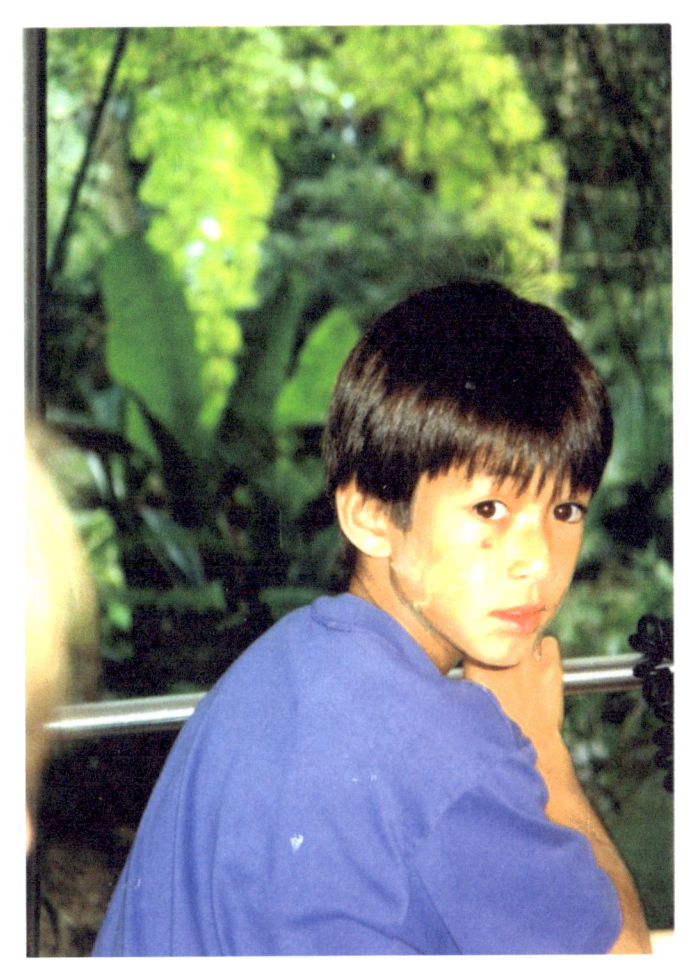

9:45—(uses booklet to look up word) "we (no cap) will have peza. in (no cap) we will have coke cake to in oth air boat."/teacher calls for students to read from journal

9:50—On task/listening to reading/reads his story/on task/continues on task

The assessor had a very busy morning following David. When deeply interested, he could stay on task. Otherwise, he was easily distracted. Still, he was eight going on nine.

No surprise, he was diagnosed with attention deficit disorder and hyperactivity. The cure: Ritalin, 5 mg. a day.

I think the wart removal may have been more successful; there was just one treatment with liquid nitrogen.

Sometime in the 1994-95 school year, the children were moved to a pre-adoptive placement that would not end well in Ft. Pierce, St. Lucie County. David was attending White City Elementary. In his record from his time there remains a sheet that lists all his Ritalin administrations. Beginning January 30, 1995, he received the drug five days a week, 5 mg. every school day at noon . . . except for April 4, 1995 when the school health aide ran out. And the administration was amazingly consistent . . . once as early as 11:40 a.m. and once as late as 12:39 p.m., but most often in the 12:08 sweet spot.

And there are other assessments of his performance. A guidance counselor at White City Elementary School noted March 3, 1995:

> David McNutt is a third grade student at our school. I have spoken with David about his progress and behavior since his arrival at WCE/ I also spoken with _____ on several occasions about his background and his needs. We are able to work with David on self-esteem issues and offer emotional support. However, we are not able to work as in-depth on his emotional needs as frequently as we feel he should be counseled.
>
> [. . .]
>
> However he does appear to need as much counseling support as could be provided.

And then she asked for outside help.

All the kids faced the challenges that come with enrollments in so many schools and with broken bonds to so many families. We didn't want to be just one more on their passage to growing up.

When they came to us, Kathy realized that one of the dangers would be school-based testing, and they would be labeled as attention-deficit disordered or worse, and those labels would follow them through the system here.

Yes, David may well have been ADHD, almost certainly suffered from ADHD, but we wanted to give him a chance to back off the diagnoses. He did not come with active prescriptions, so we didn't seek them out.

We think we know now that they were victims of post-traumatic stress disorder. All the signs were there. For example, when things would suddenly devolve . . . there was an emergency that did not initially involve them, perhaps a playground injury of another student . . . they would exacerbate the situation, begin escalating. It was like pouring gasoline on a fire.

A local Montessori school took the time to meet with us and to meet the children. It was a Godsend. And for the first year at least, it worked well. Except for the weekly call about someone acting out.

Our daughter needed remedial help in most subjects, but especially reading. She had managed to miss out on the fundamentals in her peripatetic education. And because she was so smart, she had been able to cover much of the time. She hated to be in grade-school readers, and we did everything we could to help her move ahead, but the stigma she gave herself was a challenge. She was dumb, she said, that was all. Her IQ tested at the top of the charts. (All three tested well above average intelligence.) She limped along that first year, and, during the summer, I took most mornings off from my self-employment, and we launched into Hooked on Phonics. I remember work sessions, play sessions, snacks, music . . . all three of them took piano lessons, field trips, always something to look forward to, or so we hoped.

And there were times when things just didn't go well. Shortly after they came to live with us, JungYi had been invited to stay overnight with a classmate. We were happy that she had made a friend. I was not so happy when I received a call that she had been arrested for shoplifting a pack of Maybelline Expert Eye Pencils, Maybelline Moisture Whip, and a Goudy Pony Twist, in all a $10.17 retail value. She was put on immediate probation and made a temporary ward of the court. She only put the cosmetics in her purse, she said, because the other girl asked her to. Maybe. We didn't know then, but that theft began a long series of interactions between our children and the legal system.

Of the three, Daniel was the most aware that he could get things if people felt sorry for him. Strangers would learn of all that had happened to him, and they would give him things: food and toys, especially. He liked that.

We packed lunches for all three to take to school. David and JungYi would chow theirs, trading as children do with others, but the lunch would go away as it was intended. The first intimation that something was amiss with Daniel was his returning home with his lunch still mostly full; almost always the sandwich was still there, untouched. Daniel was not especially impressed with what we sent, and he wanted something else, something more. So, he'd ditch his Power Ranger® lunchbox and stake the claim that he didn't have anything to eat.

Once Kathy got a call from the school asking if we needed financial help. Daniel had claimed that not only didn't he have a lunch for that day . . . but any day. He said we had told him that because he was only in school for six hours, he didn't need a lunch. Kathy told the school that Daniel came equipped with food each and every day. She asked if it wouldn't be odd that we'd send lunch for the other two and not include Daniel. She thanked the academic director for her concern. To Daniel she promised to not only show up with his lunch every day but to sit with him while he ate it. No, Daniel, said, that was okay; he'd eat his lunch from then on.

Over the years we received a lot of unsolicited advice from parents who had recently come into Daniel's sphere about how we should be kinder, gentler, more understanding. At least that's where they started until they'd spent a little more time with Daniel. His pity seeking was one thing in a very cute child. We knew it would be something else in a teen or an adult.

Another intimation of Daniel's character was his penchant for taking things. At visits, especially when we'd visit my late-wife's mother. There would always be something missing. And any time we found unusual things in his possession we'd make inquiries. Very often he'd say he found it . . . it didn't belong to anybody, so it was his for the taking. That led to a mantra: "You don't know whose it is, but you know whose it's not." It seemed to make no impression.

JungYi might not tell all, but she would not directly lie. And David would always tell the truth when questioned, and I don't recall any time when he took something that wasn't his.

David's most serious concerns from the time he arrived in our home were the great fears he experienced at night. He was sure there were aliens watching and they were going to come to get him. Very often he would resort to sleeping in Daniel's room, often on the floor. All three children had bedrooms on the lower level of our walkout ranch. At the foot of the yard was a little bayou just off the Grand River, the state's longest. It would be easy to imagine almost anything coming out of the swamp and up the hill to the house.

For David, those aliens with their overlarge and blank eyes, their smooth pates, their long fingers of whatever number gave rise to a fear that was real and unreasoning.

I have reflected since that perhaps we were in some measure his aliens. After all, what were we but people who came in and took him away? And it had happened before. We were just the latest in a series of what may have seemed to him as abductions.

Our religious practice was another arena that the children found strange. We are Anglicans . . . Episcopalians, I from the cradle, Kathy from a profession. I think she was raised mostly Lutheran, a close affiliate. Coming as they did from Southern Baptist tradition, the children had interesting observations. In church, on hearing a selection from the rich tradition of Bach, Mendelsohn, Charles Wesley, and hundreds of other composers, David asked, "Did somebody die?" The music was to his ear lugubrious. On seeing a woman preach, the children remarked that she couldn't do that.

And, early on there were some Sundays of absolute misbehavior by the boys in church. I remember one service where, after admonishing them to amend their behavior, I ended up removing them by picking up both of them, one under each arm, and negotiating my way out the back of church. They were laughing, and I had to admit that it must have looked pretty silly. Over time, their behavior in church vastly improved, but they always bore watching; they were children.

They had been through a lot in their early church lives, including, as very young children, the rite of exorcism, or at least the Baptist take on it. To my mind, they had been singled out, identified, and then prayed over in a fashion that makes my skin crawl . . . still. Oh, there is evil in the world, but to treat children in such a way offers little for their long-term good. We talked about it and what they thought it all meant. It was clear that they thought others viewed them as less, as damaged.

Before the adoption was finalized, we had to go before a Florida judge to give our promise that we would be parents to these children and that they agreed to be adopted. By good fortune this was handled over the telephone. We all sat around the dining room table and put the phone on "speaker."

Yes, Kathy and I understood this was forever. We promised to do our best by them. And yes, one by one the children agreed to be adopted.

The process was completed Nov. 2, 1995.

David McNutt with his three children shortly before he relinquished custody.

Our adoption of these children was semi-open. We didn't know where their mother was and were concerned what might happen if and when she'd surface. Their father knew exactly where his children were, and we took a weekly collect phone call from him. David McNutt talked with his children about how everything was going to get better, how things were coming along for him. He wanted to move up from Florida and be near us so the kids could visit him. It was going to be wonderful. Their hearts may well have wanted him much closer, but they knew he was unreliable. As long as he was sober, things were unremarkable. But when he was drinking, he exhibited clinical behavioral issues. Serious problems. He was sick from drinking, and his repeated injuries from fights had taken a toll.

We were not easy about the contact; the children sometimes would act out after a call. And Kathy and I set pretty firm lines about the interaction. We determined that contact with him was in their best interests.

The calls were not always regular. There were missed weeks and excuses.

Still, he remembered the kids at Christmas. Daniel's wish had been a pocket watch, reminiscent of the antique Elgin that I carried. David McNutt made it happen for Daniel, and I think Daniel cherishes it still. JungYi and David also got thoughtful gifts.

After a year of this remote contact, we got a call that he had died of an overdose. If I recall correctly, the news came to Kathy while the kids and I were at the YMCA. After a quick conference we decided that there could be no hesitation: we needed to fly with them to Knoxville, the family home, and where David McNutt would be buried in a military cemetery. We knew we would encounter family members, people they had known and whom we did not. It didn't matter that it might have been uncomfortable. There would be no do-over for the children.

They were plenty upset, had endless questions to which we had no answers at the time. We arrived, found our hotel and met Uncle Joe, who drove us to the funeral home. Uncle Joe was married to their father's sister Karan. Some of the family members were there when we arrived. Much was made over the children, how much they'd grown. It had been a couple years since David took them off to Florida and no one there had seen them since. There were tears.

Even after embalming, David McNutt's body was bloated. I suspected that he might have been dead some time before he was found. Still, he was recognizable to his children. Daniel especially had questions about the body, what had happened, what would happen. David listened closely. I remember after everyone moved aside that I took a picture of their father there in the casket. Some people consider it a barbaric practice. I intended it as a record, and an important one. Its purpose was to memorialize this man who had been our children's first father. The children had very few photos of him.

After the funeral home visitation we were invited back to the house where we met even more family. People wanted to know about the children's lives, about us. Uncle Joe nudged Kathy outside to talk. Later she told me about it. They wanted to know if we had come down to collect on insurance money that might have been due the family. There wasn't much, he said.

Kathy assured him we had not. Because the adoption had been finalized, the children had no rights to inherit from his estate; they were no longer his legal children. And we had no interest. No, Kathy told him, we had come down because we thought it best. Joe was relieved and the rest of our time was not under quite such wondering scrutiny.

Uncle Joe took some time to speak with me. What did I do? A writer and filmmaker? Was I going to write a book about adopting the kids? He said it seemed like a natural topic for a writer; what an adventure. I was mildly offended that he thought I'd trade on the children's lives. (Is that what I'm doing now?)

The service the next day was brief and held at the Tennessee State Veterans Cemetery. We were outside under a gazebo. Then we observed taps, a salute, and a flag folding and presentation. The burial would take place after we left. The graves were laid out in order of interment . . . there were no family plots, no privilege. Equal under the red Tennessee clay and vibrant green sod.

Afterward, back at Uncle Joe's and Aunt Karan's there was more socializing. The children reconnected with their cousins and people several generations older. And we heard stories. The children's great-grandfather had been a moonshiner and preacher. "He'd took a stroke and died" after he carried a hundred pounds of sugar over the hill to his still. Of their father's generation, half of the children had fallen into alcoholism and the last one of that number, David, had just died. The others were teetotal and well educated, had good jobs and houses. They were evident of intelligence and industry. There were risks and lessons. It was illustrative, and I hoped the children were paying attention.

My favorite of the whole family was Uncle Jerry, actually their great-uncle. We went to visit his house, and the kids managed to relax on a big tire swing. Uncle Jerry took us across the road to a cemetery where he served as sexton. That's where many in the family had been buried, including an uncle who had died in prison. It was a sad story. Very sad.

On a much brighter note, we also managed to bring the children to Granny McNutt, or as she was called, Granny Nutt, the matriarch. I think she was more than 100 years old, but she knew who these children were, and she hugged them. I remember her being very deaf, but not much impaired otherwise. It was clear that she loved them mightily.

*David gets a goodbye hug from Grannie Nutt (McNutt), **the family matriarch.***

As a last event, we stopped by the cemetery to view the closed grave.

By the time we arrived home, we were bone tired. And we were pretty sure that their biological father's death would have repercussions for them. It was one more loss.

In a matter of a few days, things were seemingly back to whatever was normal for us. That meant there would be lots of activity. All three of the kids were physically gifted in ways I never experienced as a polio child.

There is a handout in our files of a wrestling tournament. David took first place in his division (65+ pounds) and Daniel took second in his division (75+ pounds). At that time Daniel weighed more than his older brother: 77 compared to 71 pounds. And I knew from wrestling with them that they were really hard to pin down. And strong.

The boys were baseball players, all three children played soccer, and were in gymnastics, track, swimming. A Friday night might be an outing to the YMCA and the pool.

. . . Or a movie, although we had to be careful what David saw because of his Technicolor® imagination. When it came time for his retelling, Kathy and I got our ears filled. David was a long-form raconteur. He would go to a movie and then take nearly an hour at the dinner table relating the plot and all the characters, major to minor. By that point in our family life, dinner had become a time to eat and talk.

Sometimes the talk was of what happened to them. I remember one occasion when the boys were riding the local Harbor Transit. One rider suggested that they all go back where they came from.

David had asked the taunting rider if that meant Knoxville.

Another time, it was just David and a friend on the bus. David was targeted as "Mr. Wang." His tormentor called him "an Asian man," and talked to him in a contrived Asian speech. He even talked about having great Chinese food the night before.

David got up and moved to the front of the bus, but that didn't silence his critic. The bus driver not only intervened, but we got a report of the incident.

That gave rise to a discussion. Kathy and I hated that our community was sometimes cruel and crude.

All three of the children received remarks about their "exotic" appearance . . . exotic meaning in this case "not from around here." Sometimes they were praised for their Asian physical attractiveness, our daughter especially. When someone would comment to Kathy, she would say of JungYi, "Yes, and she's beautiful on the inside as well." Other times the children were castigated for not being American-looking enough. Either way…

There was music in the house, too. All three had started piano lessons. The first piano teacher was a delight. She enjoyed children, too. When you start piano lessons, there often is no way to tell whether there might be the spark of artistry there. Oh, sure, once in a while you can tell immediately, but in most cases, it takes time. In addition, both boys chose to follow me into trumpet playing.

David concentrates on the mechanics of playing. That's a nice embouchure.

I would bring them with me to select gigs—maybe playing for pre-game and seventh-inning stretches at our local Class A Midwest League West Michigan Whitecaps games at the then named Fifth/Third stadium in Grand Rapids (now LMCU Ballpark); the boys got the best of both worlds—music and baseball. And there were other local gigs when the kids got to get close to pianists, banjoists, and tuba players, all manner of music makers.

JungYi had told us early on that one of her dreams was to work as a model. Headshots, a bio, seminars . . . and boom! She was signed by Unique Models. She did a couple of shows in Grand Rapids, a few out of town, some newspaper fashion-section sessions, a couple catalog shoots. And she was pretty much done with it. There was no question in my mind that she could have gone much further; she and her brothers could have been professional models based on their looks and comfort before an audience. But there wasn't the fire. And as far as we were concerned, limited exposure to that world was better for them. But had they been alive to that, we'd have done our best to support it.

Body image may have played a part in JungYi's case. I learned to hate Howard Stern when JungYi came to us crying. She had been listening to the shock jock and heard him say that any woman who weighed more than 120 pounds was a fat pig. There is rarely any way a parent will have more authority than a media personality. We did our best to reason through the issue of the growing and maturation process and were distressed for her when that didn't help.

And to help teach responsibility, we started a chores and rewards system called Kid's Biz. That helped keep the house a little more orderly, and it made a link between daily chores and finances. Daniel was far and away the most financially savvy, and even as the youngest he often had the most money . . . and most of the time from his own honest initiative. I joked that he was Daniel the Dealer because he had such a talent for buying and selling; he could talk his playmates into deals, and they did not seem put out or misused.

The high point of my life as an adopted (and adoptive) father was reading aloud at bedtime. Early on JungYi opted out, so I would position myself on a chair in the hallway between the two boys' rooms and read. We started with very short stories and worked our way up the R. L. Stine's *Goosebumps* series. I see the books now advertised as "horror meets humor." I'd say that's a pretty apt description. Book after book, twisted plot leads to an unlikely ending. The protagonist usually lived through it all. They were inventive and fun, and Stine held the boys' attention. After a time, though, I longed to bring them an awareness of what I consider some of the best of literature.

The Lion, The Witch, and The Wardrobe was first on my list. And it worked. We went through all the Narnian Chronicles, then launched into *The Hobbit*. Then *Once and Future King*. Back for the Trilogy of the Rings. We even waded through *Pilgrim's Progress*—not a good choice. But they stuck with it, rarely falling asleep before I was done.

The Chronicles of Narnia stayed with them like no other stories. They stayed with me, too. I haven't read them in probably the last five years, but before that I would devour them, as fresh as the first time I read them. Lucy, Edmund, Peter, Susan, Eustace . . . they were the stuff of legends. We often would talk about them on trips.

In fact, on one trip David told me I needed to write a book called *The Dragon and the Rose*. It took nearly 15 years for that story to be finished, but it is now published and dedicated with love to all three of our children, but especially to him:

> *Dedication and thanks:*
>
> *This book was written with love for JungYi, Dan, and the one who first spoke the title—David. David has walked on, but he will be forever in our hearts.*

He was securely in our hearts then, too, as a boy. ...And a boy facing really big challenges. He had been identified at school as a student with some issues that warranted investigating. So, working through a private therapist, we followed up with testing.

A Personal Inventory for Children (PIC) testing early in 1996—about a half year after the adoption was finalized—that David had been referred because of what the profile scale described as:

> conduct problems and academic learning difficulties that may be relatively transitory or minor. Most of these children are restless and cannot sit still, although problems are primarily demonstrated in the classroom, where they are often described as overly talkative, continually seeking attention, disruptive, overactive, inattentive, aggressive, and easily distracted.

Yes, yes, but rarely aggressive in David's case.

Kathy and I filled out the answers to such questions as: "My child frequently has nightmares." (T), or "My child can be left home alone without danger." (F). There were a lot of questions, and even while answering them, a picture was emerging.

Further explication and interpretation revealed that David was likely to be fearful, to worry, to have difficulty sleeping, and to seek to avoid "responsibilities or to withdraw from uncomfortable situations."

Further:

> Current and/or past behavior may also suggest hyperactivity, distractibility, restlessness, or impulsivity. Similar children are often inattentive in class, do not complete homework assignments, and may require adult intervention to conform to stated limits. A limited frustration tolerance may be associated with temper tantrums, destruction of objects, projection of blame, direct expression or disruption of anger, or a lack of trust in others. Other problems may include excessive seeking of attention and approval, clumsiness, frequent accidents or fire setting.

David didn't destroy things and he didn't set fires. He was prone to accidents, but most often because he was so physically active.

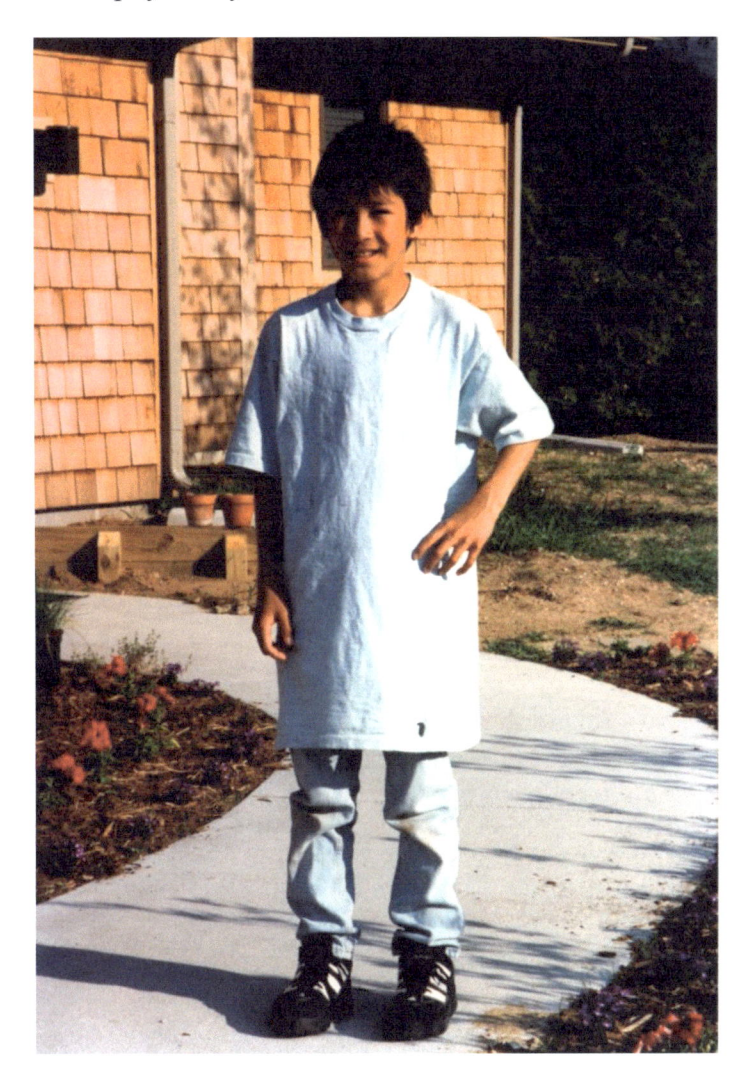

David in 1996, just outside the front door in one of my old shirts.

That was a first test. Within a few months Kathy and I also went through what was called Behavior Assessment Systems for Children's Parent Rating Scales. The test indicated that his "Behavioral Symptom Index" was in the clinically significant range, as were his "Externalizing Problems Composite" (hyperactivity, aggression, conduct problems), his "Internalizing Problems Composite" (somatization), his "atypicality," and attention problems. Additionally, he was labeled at-risk for depression, lack of adaptability, and a deficit of social skills. The test also indicated that we had a "tendency to be excessively negative in describing the child's behaviors," something that put our response in the "caution" range. The reason? Because we had answered "almost always to these questions: "Forgets things," "Daydreams," 'Is critical of others," and "Complains about the rules." We were perhaps sometimes brought up short by David's behavior, but there was no lack of love, nor did we think we were negative about him, either to him or to others. And, yes, he almost always exhibited those four behaviors.

David loved to play and said that was all he wanted to do. He didn't dream of growing up; he just wanted to stay a kid and play.

He could not stand discomfort, but neither was he willing or able to anticipate ways to forestall it. I think of him heading out of the house in chilly weather without a coat after being reminded that he should wear or bring one. Nope. Most often it didn't happen. Then he would ask someone for something to wear. One time after playing outside during the summer, he came in sweaty and cranked up the air conditioning because he was hot at that instant. Kathy explained to him that's not how things worked and turned off the air. We would remind him of anything he might want to take on any outing to keep him warm, dry, cool. When he'd neglect the reminder and begin to suffer, we eventually began to take the position that he was in charge of his own self. Next time he might remember better. Tough love with a coat? Never to his danger.

But he was so bright.

One real surprise to me was the interest that David took in the 1996 presidential election. His inclination was to support Senator Bob Dole. That may have been a reflection of my mostly Republican (at the time) sensibilities, but he took it seriously. He even had to present at the Montessori school during a debate on behalf of the candidates. Dressed in suit and tie, sporting a "Dole for President" button, he delivered a lengthy rationale for why Senator Dole should have been our next president.

David's choice was clear: Bob Dole. No one else was up to the task.

David also had the opportunity on a school field trip to see the candidate live and in person, and it made a difference. He came home with stars in his eyes. Bob Dole never had a more fervent adherent. The results of the election disheartened him. I told him we'd just have to muddle along . . . somehow.

As I write this, I can think of so many wonderful times, times when it felt that parenting was a joy. I loved doing things with the kids, something I didn't really expect when we adopted them. The first autumn they were with us, we made our way to nearby Coopersville and to the independent railroad volunteers operate with equipment that includes a locomotive, a switching engine, four passenger cars, and a caboose on a spur. The rail line runs west out of Grand Rapids toward the lakeshore. The whole operation is run by enthusiasts who also have a yard full of railroad engines and cars that are candidates for restoration. Several times a year they run their 14-mile round-trip from Coopersville to nearby Marne as theme trains: The Santa Claus train, the Easter Bunny Train. In the fall it was the Famous Pumpkin Train. Buy a ticket, get a ride AND a big pumpkin. It may have been pitched for a group a little younger than our three, but off we went along with one of JungYi's friends. I think the kids enjoyed the innocent entertainment. I did.

It's always good to have the biggest pumpkin you can carry. This one was captured at the Famous Pumpkin Train during a ride on the Coopersville and Marne Railway.

And there were other times that drove home the realization that in order to parent, you must have children who are willing to be parented. JungYi had taken a move away from familial intimacy and wanted instead just to hang with friends, a part of the natural order for young teens. But without the lifelong and firm bonds that bind most parents and children, there were greater risks. We didn't kid ourselves that any deep relationship with the children would be magical and instant. But we prayed mightily that they would come in time before the attractions that led away from the family would result in fractures.

JungYi had moved to the public junior high school and was bumping along in her classes, well-liked by teachers and friends and friends' parents, but going to the edge. We learned she had been taking Ritalin. Yes, she said when confronted, and so what? Other kids did it, too.

In a quick conversation, Kathy and I decided that it was necessary that we become ISPs . . . Industrial Strength Parents. We let JungYi know that if she thought taking drugs was a good idea, we'd make sure all her friends' parents would know we thought it was a good idea, too. And Grandma and Grandpa should know, too.

We took to meeting with the parents of her friends. We even invited a community Police Officer, Mark Reiss. He knew what had been happening on the streets, what our children were into, and the dangers some of their behavior represented. The coterie of young women we called Reiss's Pieces.

And things got worse. During one hot summer night, Kathy and I lay abed and listened to the woven wire fence on the side of the house zing as she vaulted it. I went downstairs and replaced the screen, both to keep the cat in and the mosquitos out, and I closed and locked the window. If she was planning to come back in that way after her nocturnal frolic, she'd have a challenge.

Instead, she was brought home by an officer. And then, regularly, police and sheriff's cars were rolling up the drive. She was drugging and drinking.

After one ride home I talked with the officer about the possibility of juvenile detention in our county facility. He could do that if she was a danger to herself or others. Herself? Definitely.

The juvenile facility is in one of the county buildings at the center of Ottawa County. The adult jail is in the same building, but firmly separated so there is no contact between juveniles and adults. So, too, is the Probate Court. The county offices and the sheriff's department are just down the service drive. Central dispatch is there, too, and county records storage.

Juvie is state-of-the art. The staff is trained, and each worker is chosen because she or he has a heart for the job. I remember our first visit as an eye opener for her and us. We were shepherded into one of the classrooms. Then JungYi was let in. We were there with a couple other parents and detained children. I was in tears. Is this what JungYi wanted? If she didn't, there was a way out, a way to short circuit all the trouble. And she was more than smart enough to know it.

No, she said, this wasn't what she wanted. She did her time, worked the program, and in a few weeks was out on probation.

I would later learn that it usually takes several trips before young people get the idea. (And later I would take weekly trips to juvie to read to the youngsters, figuring that the youngsters, like the boys, might be hungering for stories to be read to them, something most of them had never experienced. I did that for more than a decade and found it meaningful service. I suppose in a way, I wanted another chance to try to help someone young.)

It did take JungYi several trips. The problem, she said, was us. Everything would be better, she insisted, if she didn't have to live in the shithole we called home.

We suggested that it might be to her advantage to consider a boarding school. That way if we were the problem, she'd be away from us and could show her strengths. She didn't want to go to any boarding school. But she wanted to live someplace else.

By this point we were pretty deep in the system. She was attending mandatory substance abuse counseling when one of her friends she'd met there died of a heroin overdose. We talked with her counselor at juvie and that psychologist said of our daughter that she'd never met a young girl with such self-destructive tendencies.

Then came what were called "wrap-around" meetings: consultations with social workers, therapists, mental health workers with the county's Social Services team. Kathy filled out reams of documents. All our family life was laid out there on the table: income, expenses, observational reports. Our family was no longer only our business . . . not, come to think of it, that it ever was since we began the process of adopting our children.

Wrap-around meetings led to wrap-around services. In the end, yes, JungYi could be placed in foster care.

We tried that and JungYi rebelled when she found she wasn't the only foster child in the home. Kathy and the foster mother met, shared observations. Kathy told the foster mother just about to the day when our daughter was likely to cycle into chaotic behavior yet again.

The day came at school—and it was the high school by that point—when her behavior was badly altered. She blew a .14 blood alcohol level. Oh, and she stole a sandwich from the cafeteria.

Once more in juvie and facing the possibility of a term in the state prison for girls, we talked with her again about the idea of going to a boarding school. Yes, she'd go. She was exhausted. We were exhausted. The toll on the boys was mounting, and they were frightened for her.

What would this mean? We had long-since finalized the adoption. Would this disrupt it? Was JungYi no longer going to be our daughter? The boys were justly afraid. We were, too. Different places that would accept her had different requirements. Some of them demanded that the familial bond be legally sundered.

No, that could not be the route we'd take. She was our daughter.

State-run or certified placement is prohibitively expensive. And most other secular institutions would have beggared us in short order. Somehow it is only the fundamentalist Baptists who seem to deliver services for troubled youth. There was one place—New Creations—in Richmond, Indiana, and we could afford it . . . just. There were dorms, classes, church activities, sports. There even were day students who came in for classes. So it was well regarded by a segment of the surrounding community.

We had called for and received literature, the fee structures, case histories of young people who told their stories, endorsements from parents. Yes, we'd drive the six hours to go and see, with the possibility—the probability—that JungYi would stay there for the next few years. There were all kinds of opportunities to monitor our daughter's progress and to write to her and call her, and there were vacations at home.

She would need long dresses and other accoutrements of modest clothing.

Why is it just the Baptists? I've wondered then and since. Why do the Anglicans not believe that they can mold young lives? I love Baptists, but I am not easy among them. And I was not easy about turning over our daughter. Simply, I did not see that I had any other choice.

During her two years there, JungYi learned much about getting along. She didn't enjoy it, but I think she was humanely treated. In phone calls she would talk of small kindnesses. I know I relished the times that I would pick her up to come home and we'd celebrate Christmas or her spring break or her summer holiday. And there were a few visits there. It was a long, long way. Thanksgiving was there. We stayed at a nearby motel and for our holiday meal went to a buffet. The children stuffed themselves.

But it was clear that her situation was not well in hand. There was volatility; she was too intelligent and too determined for the situation not to chaff.

But she was safe.

That left the boys. It was not David, the next oldest, who acted out first.

Daniel had taken to bold thefts, even before JungYi left home. He stole $100 from a camp counselor and used it to buy an aluminum baseball bat at our local Meijer store. They had him on still camera paying for the $70-something bat using a single bill. He had refused to admit the theft until confronted with the picture. His apology to the camp's director and his counselor was less than genuine.

There were countless other thefts, little and large, and there was no repentance. Consequences? Didn't really matter.

For me and Kathy, there was no recourse ever to physical correction. There was no spanking or anything else that would involve swatting or hitting. It doesn't work with dogs, much less children. And these kids had suffered that kind of "correction" before. In spades. In fact, when Daniel was five or six an adult had grown so angry with Daniel that he knocked him clear across a room. Daniel had landed on his forehead; a bony knot endured beneath the small patch of scarred skin. Heaven only knew what brain damage that might have caused. Another time when Daniel was even younger, he had been locked in a closet and left there, told as the door closed that Freddy Krueger of *Nightmare on Elm Street* was coming to get him through that attic hatch above him. Then the family promptly forgot about him and went out for a day at the beach.

There was no physical measure that we could employ to improve things.

The only times Daniel was restrained was when he was thrashing. A dear friend who is an expert in holding therapy told us to bundle him and hold on. Of anything, that seemed to help when he was younger. I had some ripped tee shirts but never any ripped skin, a testament to Daniel's true intent.

But with the expansions of his thefts came an uncanny interest in crime. He talked often and at length about Seth Privacki, a teenager who shot and killed his parents, brother, brother's girlfriend and his grandfather. The crime had taken place in nearby Muskegon. Daniel couldn't quite figure out why young Privacki didn't stand to inherit. I am sure that more than once I looked askance at my youngest child.[3]

David meanwhile had moved from the Montessori school to a Catholic junior high in Muskegon, a hefty drive away. Of all the area educational institutions, we judged that Muskegon Catholic Central was far and away the best choice. The administrators and teachers there were willing to work with David if he wanted to work with them. And one of David's friends also went there. We'd get up early, pick up his friend and drive over the bridge above the Grand River to a bank parking lot in nearby Ferrysburg, where a bus would come down from Muskegon to pick up local kids. Miss that bus, and it involved making the 30-mile round trip.

Daniel had moved to Grand Haven Christian elementary. He was an able student, but again and again he was disciplined for thefts.

---

[3] Privacky was himself shot and killed during an attempted prison break in 2010.

I repeatedly told him that if I couldn't trust him out of my sight he wasn't getting out of my sight. So, we spent a lot of time together. And we began cautionary tales of boarding school. He wouldn't like it, I told him, and I didn't want him to go there. No, he wouldn't be going where JungYi was attending. Instead there was a boarding school in Lucedale, Mississippi, Bethel Boys Baptist Academy, run by Brother Herman Fountain. Military discipline led by former soldiers. We had a brochure, we had talked about the possibility with Brother Fountain. We had talked with other parents. But it was a long ways away, and it was expensive. We'd be using money we had set aside for their college education; JungYi was chewing hers up at a pretty good clip. And here's where we'd start with Daniel. Every dollar that went to a boarding school would be one less for any higher education; we simply didn't have it.

I begged him to stop his thievery. But there came a point. I had talked with the principal at Daniel's school. His academic performance was fine, better than fine when he was interested in the subject, but his thefts were disrupting his class. He was on the verge of expulsion.

I sat him down: "The next time you steal something you are going to be tossed out of that school. At that point we are on your way to Bethel Boys," I told him, Kathy in concurrence. For how long, he asked? I didn't know. It would depend.

Of course. Here was the sand, here was the line in the sand. It might have been two days before he was caught stealing a Blow-Pop, a piece of candy, from another student's desk. The principal called and said that Daniel was no longer welcome at the school. Did we want to send him to the local public school? No, we told him. We were going to move him south, instituting the plan we had discussed.

The night before the trip, Kathy was on edge. Something didn't feel right, she said, and she swept through the kitchen, taking every knife from the drawers and putting them in the safe in our bedroom. My sharp tools were already under lock and key in the garage.

I still have the tickets. Issued for December 11, 1999. Schock, David, and Schock, Daniel, had train seats from nearby Holland, Michigan, to Chicago, and from there to New Orleans. From New Orleans we were to train to Mobile, Alabama. It didn't work out exactly that way; we were bussed on the last leg of our journey.

Had it been other circumstances I think it would have been an adventure, and maybe it was for Daniel. We stayed in a nice hotel in Mobile. I rented a car, and we drove and drove and drove to the back of beyond. I was later to read of the place as a hellhole with instructors little better educated and disciplined than their charges. And those charges! A goodly number of them were kids just warehoused as adoptive parents took in adoption subsidies. Some of the youngsters were truly disturbed. But others were just there as a result of parents having run out of options for kids who were acting out.[4]

---

[4] We did receive an adoption subsidy from the state of Florida. It was a help, but was nowhere near enough to cover the expenses of raising, educating, and providing for these three children. We wanted them to have rich lives.

Brother Fountain answered all my questions and a few from Daniel, who was sitting with us for the first part of the session. He was then taken to tour the facility, to get into his uniform. And then I'd see him as a new soldier before I left. Any drugs he was on? They'd be stopped immediately; they didn't believe in pharmacology. How bad is his acting out? What had we tried in terms of correction? What about faith?

I explained that although the children had been raised in the South Baptist tradition for the first years of their lives, Kathy and I were Anglicans, and we had been taking the children to our local Episcopal Church services.

"We'll give him something very familiar," said Brother Fountain. I said I trusted that did not mean corporal punishment. "No, that doesn't work," Brother Fountain affirmed. "But he'll be in church, in a good, ol' Baptist service. We bus in the girls from our sister school in Hattiesburg, and it just makes a nice Sunday. And we watch everybody and everything."

Discipline, discipline, and programmed school lessons from a commercial curriculum. It was not my first choice for my son. When he came to say goodbye, he had begun to understand his situation. His head had been shaved and he was in a cadet's uniform.

"How long will I be here?"

For now, a year. That was the plan. But it would depend.

That night back at the hotel, Kathy called and relayed something that David had said. Daniel and one of his friends had planned to murder Kathy and maybe me, too. Evidently, the thinking was that Daniel and David could get the insurance money, and they could just live in the house without grownups.

This was probably the hardest thing David ever told, and it may account for much that followed. In telling us, he betrayed his own brother. Kathy may have saved her own life and mine, but David confirmed the danger.

Daniel was 13 years old. I have known of other youngsters that age and younger who have killed. Kathy and I took this seriously. At that point, I doubted that Daniel was ever coming home to stay.

On my way back north to return to Grand Haven, I found myself waiting in Chicago's Union Station. I almost never travel without at least a pocket trumpet, compact and easily packed, to practice. I listened to a Salvation Army group struggle for a time with their selections of seasonal and sacred music before I asked if they wanted some help. They did. They said it was joyful to have another lead brass voice. For me the act of playing was a sorrow, needful, but a lament. At last I got on my train to ride back to Michigan.

Over the months, Daniel called and would beg to return to Grand Haven. I knew that he wouldn't be coming home in the foreseeable future. While keeping us safe was part of the equation, the other part was we wanted to minimize the chances that Daniel would do something so violent that for all intents and purposes his life would be ruined, like Seth Privacky's. I was pretty sure I could defend Kathy and myself—at that point I was in my mid-40s, physically fit, about 220 pounds, and 6'3"—but we needed to make sure that he didn't have the opportunity. . . . In answer to his plea I equivocated; I felt like I wasn't telling him the entire truth. I wasn't.

He went on to talk about DI Knott—Drill Instructor William Knott. He was Daniel's role model there, the one to please to avoid punishment.[5] It wasn't hard, Daniel said, but occasionally he'd slip up and then there would be pencil rolls down the hill. And he was learning to box. Brother Fountain? Oh, he was something more than just a role model; he was an inspiration and a Godly man.

In 2000 we were spending upwards of $4,000 a month on places to keep our children safe. That number didn't go down for a long time. And it was a good thing that I found full-time employment teaching in the Communication Department at Hope College in the late summer of 2000. The regular paychecks were needed.

But our family was truly fractured. The failure of it sat deep in my stomach, the loss of JungYi and Daniel from our table and their beds, deep in my heart.

I had urged Brother Fountain to watch Daniel's cycle . . . he was able to maintain for a couple of months at most, but then something would trigger unwanted behavior. In this case at Bethel Boys', Daniel stole a car with another student, winding up in New Orleans where a railway detective halted them. That detective called to accuse Kathy and me of lax parenting, letting our son roam about and wind up in a truly dangerous city. Kathy asked him if the boys had told him that they'd stolen the car in which he'd stopped them, that they had been enrolled at a military boarding school and had run away, and that the law was looking for them? No, he guessed that Daniel had left out that part. They were transported back to Bethel, where, for a short while, he followed protocol.

Eventually he stole yet another car with yet another student. (I do wish people would stop leaving their keys in the ignition to facilitate this kind of easy access.)

After he got caught in the second vehicle the judge sentenced him to four months at a Mississippi state training camp. I wrote to him in response to a phone call. He wanted O-U-T.

---

[5] William Knott would in 2015 be identified as one of three perpetrators of abuses at a Mobile school, Saving Our Youth Foundation. They were arrested after a grand jury indictment.

Sunday, Oct. 8, 2000

Dear Daniel:

Where do I start? I almost don't know. I don't know what to say to you; I can't think of anything that really will help. But I'll write to you and even if I don't say anything very good, at least it's a start.

I would guess that after Bethel Boys' this state camp is probably not too difficult. Still, you need to know that if you screw up there, Mississippi WILL put you in a youth prison. Maybe that's where you want to go.

I'd also guess that you're picking up all kinds of education about stealing, fighting, lying, cheating . . . the place where you are now is probably full of people you like.

Oh, my son. This is what happens when you decide to follow evil instead of good. And you have chosen a very bad path to follow. . . . All of which makes you a very dangerous young man. I thank God that you did not kill anyone with either of the two cars you stole. All the damage that you've done to other people and their property will have to be paid for. That falls to Mom and me, even if we don't have the money to do it. I did warn them after you stole your first car that you were most likely to steal another, but they didn't see fit to put you under lock and key as I suggested. Now they understand and it will be some time before you taste freedom again.

If you are able to go the ten weeks without another episode of defiance, Brother Fountain said he will take you back for six months. Steal another car, truck, van, or anything else, and you will be breaking parole and go right into prison.

And, why? Why is it you need to do this? What are you trying to prove? That nobody can tell you what to do? Take a look around. You should find yourself with lots of other kids who won't let anybody tell them what to do, either. And where are you? In a place where you are told what to do . . . minute by minute. The loss of freedom is a terrible tragedy. You have traded yours for a handful of stupid thefts here, major thefts in Lucedale, and an attempt to escape from the law. Was it worth it? Are you happy? Is this the life you choose? If you like it . . . you're on the right track.

And if you don't like it . . . you are the ONLY person who is going to be able to change it. And it will take time . . . probably years. Do you think anyone who knows you would trust anything you have to say about changing . . . that you're good now and not bad? Sorry, that record was worn out a long time ago.

For our part, Mom and I pray for you every day. I think of you often and wonder how you are doing. I am very sad that you choose to break the law, the rules. But, in the end, you are the one who has to pay the price. I promise you that Mom and I will NOT rescue you from the consequences of your own actions. The only way you will learn, it seems, is from your own mistakes. I pray you begin now.

He begged that he might come back to Grand Haven. I replied with a harsh letter, perhaps the most unkind letter I've ever written. I am not proud of it:

October 28, 2000

Dear Daniel:

I have reread your letter several times and each time I am sad that you do not yet understand what you have done. I'll try to explain yet again. You ask for one more chance.

Let's see . . . when did you use up your one more chance? I think about your lies. . . your almost constant lies and thefts. Maybe you used up your one more chance when you spent the week copying the verse a thousand times when you were caught in a bald-faced lie? Maybe, instead, it was when you told me on the shores of Lake Michigan while we were vacationing on Beaver Island that stealing Uncle Corey's $100 was the most stupid thing you'd ever done and nothing like that was ever going to happen again? Or, maybe it was when you were involved with David K_____ in the candy theft at camp? Or, maybe it was stealing from Grandma and Grandpa Stephenson, or Grandma Neville? Or stealing from me and mom? Maybe it was even in the face of my promise to you that the next theft would land you in Bethel Boys and you went ahead and had to steal a stupid trinket that was worth maybe fifteen cents. Do you remember me telling you that you would NOT like what happened next? I do. Do you remember me pleading with you to change your ways, begging you to give up stealing and lying? Do you remember me telling you that I could not trust you and that was sad? Do you remember me telling you that if I couldn't trust you out of my sight, you wouldn't get out of my sight? In a sense you are still in my sight for we're paying someone else to watch you.

And you wonder when you are coming home. Well, had I known then what I know now about your plans to kill Mom, I would never have left you with the impression that your stay would be for only a year (and that only contingent upon your changing your ways). No, I found that out after you were in Mississippi. And, add to all that, instead of prayerfully and genuinely seeking forgiveness and bearing a contrite heart you decided to run away and steal, to be involved in sex play far more times than you've been caught, and then—on top of all that—to steal not one but TWO cars.

And, let's see . . . you want another chance? Wake up, boyo! You've had your one more, two more, four more, five hundred more chance. The fact that Mom even says that she'd consider having you back in this home again AFTER you have spent a year behaving (starting from when you leave prison) strikes me as overly generous.

I look at it this way: You have proven yourself untrustworthy so many times that I doubt I will ever be able to trust you. If you really mean it and are sorry . . . gee, you'll have a rough next three years until you are an adult. That's too bad. If, however, you don't mean it . . . Mom could wind up dead. And afterward you'd say (again) that you didn't mean for that to happen. Sorry, I'm not gonna allow that . . . even if it means you are having a rough time. Just remember who it was who plotted to kill her, who lied, who stole, who behaved with absolute defiance of our authority over you. This was all your choice.

Let me share with you what you have thrown away so far:

A family who loved you
A musical education
A college education
The trust of anybody who knows you
Your freedom
Your future.

But this is what you asked for. Now you have it and you don't like it. Well, YOU are the only one who can do anything about it. . . . And it's going to take a long, long time.

I pray for you every day. I think about you all the time, because, even while you will never be eligible to inherit under our will (once Mom and I are dead and gone), you are still my son. I had much better hopes for you, that you would chose life and freedom and real happiness. Maybe someday you will do that. That's between you and God. But between you and me, you've used up your one more chance.

Love,

Had he really used up one last chance? It was darned clear I was angry with him. I've found since that that kind of anger evaporates at the merest suggestion that the child is doing better. At that point I was getting dad lessons, but perhaps at his expense. No, there would be other chances. And while it was true his freedom was constrained and that most of the money set aside for his college education had been drained, his future remained a possibility of healing and health. Always. I think I knew that.

And who the heck was I writing to? Could he even read the letter, much less understand it? It might have been better if he had not. There would be other letters over the years that were more encouraging. But we had learned that with Daniel, we had to be careful of what we said and wrote. He had a penchant for manipulation and would try to use anything to gain foothold. We told him regularly that we loved him. We had to learn to not react when he tried to use that against us. Sometimes it was wearing. It led to a certain distance and caution, something you never want to experience with a child . . . who is, after all, a child.

The message in the letter had to be unambiguous but it could have been more loving. There was no way he was coming home to live in the near future. Of course, that wasn't a worry for the next ten weeks, well into 2001.

And, through all Daniel's challenges, David found himself alone and unmoored.

At Muskegon Catholic Central, he was inattentive and disruptive in class, lacked self-control, was failing some quizzes, was careless in his written work. On occasion he would show improvement, but in his eighth-grade year—after Daniel went to Bethel Boys'—it was downhill.

He started missing the bus home, or acting out and being sent home. That meant a lot of trips during the workday to retrieve him.

And the infractions ranged from minor to major. One of the least was "[f]orging Mom's signature to previous disciplinary report." That required a Saturday in-school suspension . . . and the round trips of about 60 miles to make it so.

Far more serious was a report of harassment:

> David made remarks and comments about sex during a break in band on Monday. When asked by his teacher to stop talking like that, David continued. It was also reported by students that he was doing a "humping" behavior on another student's backpack (David reports he was only shaking the backpack.)

That really wasn't a good sign. For David, at the end of the school year, we decided that as much as we loved Catholic Central and all it stood for, there was no way we could continue the process. In part, David had made himself a less-than-desirable student.

So, our remaining plan for David was that he would be enrolled in the local public school for the fall.

At 16 he was discovering drugs and alcohol with friends. He had fallen in with a crowd of young people who seemed aimless. He started public school with indifferent results. One of his aims was to do as little work as possible. He wanted to join friends in the special education classes because he thought they didn't have to do much work.

And he was running the streets. At one point in the car after picking him up, I asked him what he wanted, what was wrong? I knew that he had depended on Daniel, and with Daniel gone and JungYi gone, there really wasn't much for him. He was a ghost. He gave no answer. So, I repeated my questions.

"Just fuck you, Dad," he shouted.

I told him it was good that he could say that. I was glad to know how he felt. Still it wasn't likely to change things.

And he became verbally abusive to Kathy. When I wasn't around his backchat was threatening. Kathy was not one to be intimidated, but she noted it. Her sister, Barb, had come to spend her last months with us. She was dying of cancer. Having her in the house may have put extra pressure on everybody, but it was a chance to do Barb the service of not having to live her last months in a nursing home or, at the last stages of her illness, in hospital. Barb had most recently worked as an emergency room nurse at Henry Ford Hospital. She had lived her life driving fast cars, riding Harleys, and early on had worked as a bartender at Detroit's famed Baker's Keyboard Lounge. She was tough, and she was smart. There wasn't much that could frighten her. But she said David's behavior was threatening.

Kathy's brother John had a household of a daughter and two sons in Windsor, Ontario. John was between jobs, and with our financial support, he said he would be happy to take on David's care, giving him a change of scene and the opportunity to hang out with kids close to his age. He would go to high school there.

David thought that would be cool. He could smoke all he wanted to, something he couldn't do at home. He went. He was 16.

Daniel Leaves Bethel Boys'

Brother Fountain was willing to have Daniel back for a time after he served his time at the training school, but the judge said, "Get that-there boy out of this-here county."

Someplace else, but where?

Kathy's sister died March 19, 2001, just before I was scheduled to go down and visit Daniel and talk about what might be next for him. Kathy held off the funeral for one day, so that I could get there and back, the 20th and the 21st.

I remember sitting with Daniel on some bleachers, and he cautioned me to look out for black widow spiders that lived on the underside of the wood planks.

His shoes were spotlessly shined, spit shined, he said. He had learned a lot about that. After the training school, Bethel Boys' looked pretty okay. The school was okay, the food was okay, the kids were okay. Couldn't he just stay there? And if not, couldn't he just come home?

No.

It would take me some time, I said, until Mom and I could make a decision about where was next for him. He had to move.

Brother Fountain knew pretty much all the other schools like his, and he recommended two, both Baptist, both in Missouri, a state we subsequently learned was noted for its lax private-school oversight.

The summer of 2001, I went to tour them both. The best, I thought, was Mountain Park Academy run by Brother Sam Gerhardt. I thought it was a step up from Bethel Boys' Academy. Certainly the buildings were better built and maintained. And the facilities near Poplar Bluff were co-educational.

Daniel was transported there and for a time things went well.

JungYi Leaves for California

Some time in all of that, maybe before, maybe after, JungYi was a passenger in a car stolen by one of her classmates. They had broken out of the dorm and run for it. JungYi had made a friend there, a boyfriend, and he had been sent home to California. Maybe JungYi had been heading there when they were arrested. The police demanded that Kathy appear before them in two hours, or they would swear out a warrant for her arrest. She explained that we were six hours away, and as a lawyer, she knew that they'd need to show cause. She had not abandoned her child.

At 17, JungYi was in that grey area. If she ran away, police would not look very hard for her. Kathy talked with her. What did she want? She wanted to go to California to be with her boyfriend, Curtis. Kathy needed to know more. Who was he, where was he? Who were his family?

Kathy made some quick phone calls. Yes, Curtis' mother would welcome her, treat her like a daughter, watch over her. Yes, she'd be in the same household with her boyfriend. It might be awkward, but there wasn't much choice. We would pay the expenses. Kathy called JungYi and told her that she would buy her a bus ticket there, that Curtis's mother was willing to help her. This woman probably saved our daughter.

While living with Curtis, his mother, and her second husband, JungYi received the kind of support that worked for her. She went back to high school and earned her diploma, not a GED. She started on training to be a home health aide.

In time, she and Curtis were married. She has found that she is an excellent mother of two of our four grandchildren, a resourceful and hard worker, honest, sober. She has created a life from what was too often chaos. She and Kathy would talk and text frequently. Our trips to southern California are not so frequent. Kathy has been there three times, I just twice. (A back injury and resulting spinal fusion made traveling impossible for me for several years.)

We are so proud of her. Do we have the right? Maybe not. But at the very least, we are so pleased that she has made this life for herself, and we are grateful to every person who contributed. So many people helped.

David at 16 was at that age when it was important to be cool and be part of a group that accepted him.

Unfortunately, that was a group whose members were messing with drugs and alcohol. He had seen firsthand the result of alcoholism and drug abuse in his father's life, but the pull was strong. We'd later learn that he was drinking and drugging pretty much every day.

David Has Trouble in Windsor

All three of the children had an easy facility for making friends. At Brother John's, David had attracted a small group. One time, John overheard David telling them of the pigsty he'd been living in with us. It was the usual hellhole description. John asked Kathy for some photos of the house, and the next time David launched into his description, John asked him if the house he was referencing was the one in the photos that he was handing about. His friends were nonplussed. John reported that they thought it looked like a nice place along the river. David was furious.

And though David stayed with brother John and his family for more than ten months, there was a limit. He couldn't maintain because of his drinking, so he found himself in a detox facility. He wanted out, and he wanted to go away, someplace.

"Where do you want to go? What do you want to do?"

He wanted to live on his own and have us pay for it. That was most unlikely, certainly not in Canada. Kathy knew more about the ins-and-outs of the social services system, she knew some of the resources available, and what she didn't know, she learned. I was tied up teaching and much of what happened sailed right past me as she exercised responsibility on both our parts for our son. We talked with him about a locked facility, something to keep him safe. But upon reflection, no, that wouldn't be a good idea for him.

So Kathy wrote him an assessment of where things stood and a detailed list of options that he could consider:

February 1, 2002

Dear David—

Dad and I have put a lot of thought and research into this letter because we love you and want you to be safe. It is a long letter because we think you and the decisions you are about to make are important. After talking about it together and praying about it, Dad and I have decided that we are no longer interested in transporting you to a locked facility. We also talked about how, when JungYi thought she was ready to be on her own, she handled her own needs and never called to say she was cold or hungry. After multiple arrests for alcohol and substances as a juvenile, she asked to be in a program that would help her with her alcoholism and help her get ready for adulthood. We made arrangements. She has now been clean and sober for some time and her life is better, even if some days are not a piece of cake. We think that you might also find that being on your own is not as easy as you expect, that not having rules may not solve all your problems, and that substance abuse plays more of a role in your problems over the last two years than you are currently able to see or willing to admit. Keep JungYi's experience in mind as you think about flying solo.

We want to encourage you as you go through this process. We hope you find among these choices several that will help you create for yourself the life you want and deserve. Your biological sister and brother have now completely turned their lives around after struggling with behaviors similar to what you are doing right now. They came from the same experiences you did and faced the same challenges personally. After trying on the life your bio-dad picked for himself (substances/jail), they both decided they didn't like that life. They wanted a different life and picked a different path. Dad and I are feeling so blessed that both of them are now being successful in their new lives.[6] We believe you can be successful, too, if you decide to and are willing to work hard at it every day to get there. We hope that at some point you will choose to make a commitment to change and work at it every day (even those days when you don't "feel like it"). Your sister and brother are both truly HAPPY now! Being on the streets and drugging did not bring your bio-dad much happiness. The changes your brother and sister have made make it very clear that it is possible for you to have a different life also. We may not be willing to do exactly what you want, but we will do what we believe will help you become a responsible adult. They both said to us recently that at one time they thought we were just being "mean" when we made decisions about ways to help them. Both of them are saying, very strongly, that now they get it—it was not punishment but a way to help them even though it wasn't what they wanted at the time. And both JungYi and Daniel are now saying how very grateful they are that we could see further up the road than they could. As we did with both of them, we will continue to be there to help you, but the help we offer may not be what you want or think you need.

---

[6] At the time Daniel was behaving far better. It was not permanent.

As you finish your time at the Detox center, this is our understanding of your current goals and here are the options that we are willing to agree to at this time (until you are legally an adult at age 18 when you will be on your own). Most of these options are based on and respect your currently stated goals of (1) wanting to get a job, (2) wanting to get your own place, and (3) wanting to "be on your own." Some are based on the possibility that you may decide you need additional support until you are 18.

These options were chosen based on the choices we have seen you make in the past two years. In the letter we wrote to your counselor before you went to live with Uncle John, we identified four issues that made it impossible for you to continue to live at our home: (1) illegal behavior (smoking cigarettes, doing drugs, internet porno, forging my signature on documents, etc.), (2) verbal abuse and threats towards me (which you denied at first, then recognized and changed for a short time), (3) refusal to attend school or comply with the rules (skipping, refusal to do detention, etc.), and (4) refusing to cooperate with curfew rules at home by leaving the house after we had gone to bed. I am attaching a copy of the letter I wrote to V____ back then to refresh your memory. After we entered into an agreement that you would change (and I also made some changes based on what you saw as a problem), you said you did not want to keep our agreement anymore. You were offered a choice of boarding school or Uncle John's, and you chose Uncle John's after staying with him for two weeks. At the time, Uncle John had the same expectations about 1, 2, and 3, (except for cigarette smoking, which you can legally do in Canada at age 16—unlike the U.S) and fewer rules than we did. You picked his home over boarding school. From what Uncle John tells me, you are now having just about the same problems at Uncle John's that you had at our home, and he is no longer willing to tolerate them.

Since you are now 17, you have some different options. I suggest you read all the options that follow and then think carefully about your decision. Once you decide which one is your first choice, you will have to write your choice down on paper and explain why (give at least three reasons) you are choosing this option. You then need to give the paper to Uncle John. I want to see in your written statement that you are doing some adult planning that supports your belief that you are ready to handle your own life. Uncle John and I will then begin to plan for your return to the United States, which may take a couple weeks, if we think your reasons are sound. Plans will be made after Uncle John has received a <u>written</u> statement with your reasons and there will be a time delay for planning after you make your decision. We will give you maps, addresses, and phone numbers to help you successfully complete the plan.

<u>If you wish to stay in Canada or you need more time to think</u>:

1. You may voluntarily enter Brentwood [Brentwood Recovery Home, a treatment facility in Windsor] for at least 21 days. Uncle John will transport you. Once you have completed that program, you will return to the U.S. and we will help you get

there. If you pick this option, you will need to decide which of the following options in the United States you want when you finish the program.

<u>If you are actually ready to go to work and support yourself, here are your choices</u>:

2. Uncle John will drop you off at the Harbor Light in Detroit [the Salvation Army facility for recovery from drug and alcohol abuse]. You can ask to stay there while you apply for welfare and then look for a job. You will be able to do whatever you are able to arrange from there. I worked there for several years, and it is a nice place with kind people. They have several different programs, a bed for the night and dinner, a substance abuse program, a hotel, and other things.

3. Uncle John will drop you off at welfare in Detroit and you can apply. They may or may not have any emergency housing, so I do not know if you will be on the streets while you wait for them to make a decision on your application. You will need to find your own resources for housing and food while you wait. Again, I suggest the Harbor Light.

4. Uncle John will drop you off at the Job Corps in Detroit. As a homeless person, you can apply for job training. If they accept you will have to wait a while (I don't know how long), they will give you free room, board, health insurance, and train you for one of a number of jobs that pay more than minimum wage. You will need to find your own resources for housing while you wait for their decision. I again suggest the Harbor Light.

5. Uncle John will take you to the bus station in Detroit and we will provide a one-way bus ticket to Holland, Michigan. You will need to make your own way to the Holland City Mission (about a 2 mile walk) and stay there until you find a job. Then you can get and pay for your own place and food. If you have trouble making ends meet, you can try applying for welfare. I again suggest the Harbor Light.

6. Uncle John will take you to the bus station in Detroit and we will provide a one-way ticket to Holland, Michigan. You will need to make your own way to the Holland City Mission, and stay there while you apply for welfare. This provides you with a place to stay while you are waiting.

7. Uncle John will take you to the bus station in Detroit and we will pay for a one-way ticket to Holland, Michigan. You will need to make your own way to the Holland City Mission. While you are staying there, you can call the Barnabas Ministry to talk about making arrangements to live in one of their homes for 17-year-olds who cannot live at home with their parents. We will help you make arrangements to get to Zeeland for the required interview and, as they require, we will attend that meeting. If you decide you will not participate in the Barnabas program, you can look for a job or apply for welfare while staying at the Mission.

8. Uncle John will take you to the bus station in Detroit and we will pay for a one-way ticket to Grand Rapids. You will then need to call The Bridge and find your way to their office. They have a voluntary program for homeless teenagers ages 17-21. They have a place for you to stay for 14 days, help with getting a job, help with getting an apartment once you have a job, and will give you some stuff for your apartment. You may be able to get in the same day if they have openings. If you have to wait to get in, you can check into the possibilities of the Salvation Army or The Guiding Light Mission (which has some meals, too).

9. Uncle John will take you to the bus station in Detroit and we will pay for a one-way ticket to Grand Rapids. You then need to find your own way to get to the welfare office or Job Corps office. I am not sure, but the Guiding Light Mission may offer beds for the night and food while you are waiting for the decision on your application at either place. We will provide the addresses for these places but you will have to get yourself there from the bus station.

10. Uncle John will take you to the airport in Detroit. We will fly you to Mobile, Alabama. They will pick you up at the airport and you will voluntarily begin a program that gets high school drop-outs ready to pass the test you have to pass to get into military service. This is not a high school academic program. They also train people to do construction (a good paying job) so they have job skills if they decide not to go into the military. The advantage of this choice is that it is warm there all year round. All your housing, food, and clothing will be provided for you plus some spending money. They only take new students on Monday.

Another option based on not working:

11. Uncle John will take you to the bus station in Detroit. We will buy a one-way bus ticket to Richmond, Indiana. Someone will pick you up at the bus station. You will voluntarily enroll at New Creations Boarding School. Since you have been there before to see Jung Yi, I don't need to explain this one further. This will be a high-school program that will help you finish the ninth grade. The teaching is a lot like the PASS program in Windsor in which you were going to enroll. All food, clothing, and shelter will be provided for you as well as some spending money.

Not an option:

You asked Uncle John to "drop you off in downtown Detroit." This is not acceptable. Detroit is a dangerous place (I lived there many years and I know), you don't know anyone there, and you don't know your way around.
Living in a cardboard box when it is so cold in a city like Detroit is a lousy and dangerous plan. If you want to be in Detroit, you need to pick one of the other places. I suggest Harbor Light where I used to work for several years—they're nice, nice people there.

Other Things You Should Know about what we will and won't do:

1. We will not provide transportation to any place other than those described in 1-11 (based on the overall plans listed above). Grand Haven has no Mission to stay at so it is not an option. I called Dockside Galley and they said they did not have a job for you.

2. We will not provide any money directly to you for an apartment, food, or living expenses. If you pick any of options 2-9, we will not provide any money (for any reason) or food (or other items) directly to you while you are waiting for your welfare to go through which is why you need to be somewhere that has a mission to stay at. We WILL financially support you by making payments directly to welfare until you are 18 if you choose to collect welfare instead of working. Welfare will contact us to make arrangements for these payments if they put you on welfare. You want to be aware that welfare has changed a lot since you were a small child and your bio-dad was collecting welfare. Because of a change in federal law, welfare in all states now requires that you work a certain number of hours a week, go to school a certain number of hours a week, be in a job training program, or go to drug treatment in order to get benefits. Be aware that if you go to a new state (other than Michigan), you may have to live there 30 days before you are eligible for welfare.

3. If you pick options 1, 10, or 11, we will be giving some spending money to you.

4. All of the following people have already told me that you may not stay at their house: Curtis and Jung Yi, Aunt Karan and Uncle Joe, Betsy and Paul, Laurie and Brian, Uncle John, and us.

5. Once you are settled somewhere, I will make arrangements to send you your personal items that are here. Do not come to our house. We will stay in touch and will come to see you wherever you are. If you choose to come anyway, I will call for a peace officer and will wait until he or she arrives before opening the door. If there is any door kicking or smashing, property damage of any type, or threats, at any time, we will press criminal charges and at 17 you will be treated as an adult, not a juvenile. You will not be allowed to stay at our house. You can avoid problems by not coming here.

6. We will be happy to accept a collect call from you once every week and would like to know how you are doing if you decide you want to at any time. As you have learned from your last two calls, we will hang up if you begin swearing or threatening. Because you are still a minor, we will also hear from the places where you apply for services generally.

7. I believe you are now too old for foster care, but you are welcome to ask for this if you think it would be helpful.

8. You may be interested to know that I called Ottawa County Child Protective Services, explained our situation, and have included the options they suggested in this letter. They already know about you in case you call them.

I look forward to hearing what choice you make and your reasons for your choice. If you have any questions, give them to Uncle John and he will discuss them with me.

Love from Mom and Dad

I read, suggested some edits, and then signed the final draft of the letter, agreed completely that it was both thorough and necessary. Looking back on it now, I wonder if David even read it or was able to read it in his drugged state (even after ten days of detox). But we knew time was running out, and he would be discharged in short order.

We anticipated that it was within David's skill set to call Child Protective Services here in our home county to complain of what he saw as our harsh and unfair treatment.

So that same day Kathy wrote to CPS:

February 2, 2002

Ottawa County Children's Protective Services
12265 James Street
Holland, Michigan

Dear L_____:

I initiated contact with you yesterday regarding my son David Schock. We adopted David and his two full siblings in 1995 at the ages of 9, 10, and 13. David is now 17 (DOB 1-15-85; SS #) and a substance abuser for at least two years. He admits to marijuana but denies other drugs; we seriously doubt this is full disclosure. He is two credits short of finishing the ninth grade, refusing to go to school, and says (at this moment) that he wants to go to work (that may change). He is currently in the City Detox Center in Windsor, Ontario, after choosing to live with my brother the past year. Because of my son's volatile and threatening behavior and illegal activities (both in our home and my brother's home), my husband and I do not feel it is safe for him to be in our home, and my brother will not agree to take him back unless he enters a 21-day treatment program which he is refusing to do. We are now in the process of making other arrangements for him.

David is refusing all boarding school options we have offered saying he doesn't want to have any rules. Based on my conversation with you, I have supplied him with a copy of the attached list of options. I am initiating this self-referral based on the expectation that he will apply for welfare and allege neglect because we refuse to give him cash. We are unwilling to give him money directly because he immediately purchases drugs. We will be happy to financially support him by making payments directly to welfare until he turns 18. I am enclosing a copy of the letter we have sent to him outlining his options.

My goal is to work with you to achieve safety for and appropriate treatment for our son. We have been actively involved in an almost identical situation with my daughter, but had the advantage of adjudication in the juvenile court system with her. N____ B_____ from Juvenile Court (her Probation Officer) and D__ S____ from CMH (Wraparound) will be able to provide you with detailed information about how hard we worked (with a successful outcome) to get help for our daughter JungYi. Mrs. F____ from Grand Haven High School also worked with us extensively while David was a student there until last February, during which time he had almost daily problems. I also spoke with R___ E____ from CMH regarding resources for our son. I have also spoken with J__ W_____ at MDCH, who says there are no appropriate treatment programs in the state for David. Some of the resources listed are based on recommendations from R___. David has had counseling at Psychological Services, psychiatric evaluation at Pine Rest Christian Mental Health Services (diagnosed with ADHD and conduct disorder) with Wellbutrin prescribed (now refusing). He is on our Priority Health insurance, but he <u>does not have Title IV-E Medicaid</u> (due to failure to apply timely when he was in foster care); he does have Florida Medicaid. We also receive $480 per month SS Survivor's benefits from his biological dad's account and $364 a month in adoption subsidy. He has $371 in a protected savings account in Grand Haven that belongs to him. The college fund he once had has been spent paying school tuition (about $475 a month U.S. funds), health insurance (required for school enrollment—about $500 a year U.S.) and room, board, and supervision in Canada over the last year (at a rate of $1,000 per month U.S.), and other personal needs. I have full documentation of money orders for these expenditures. David thinks we should pay this amount to him, which we will not.

Please feel free to contact me at your convenience. I am an attorney, a social worker under contract with the State of Michigan, and a student at Western Theological Seminary. My husband is a visiting professor at Hope College. Because of our professional situations, we prefer to take a proactive stand on this situation. I will be most happy to discuss any additional ideas or suggestions you have as well as any concerns. Thank you for your time and attention.

Sincerely,

Kathy Neville [phone number]

In the end he said he wanted to go to Florida. He'd liked it when he lived there before. He was just going to live on a beach. Kathy did some quick connecting. All right, we said. John will buy a bus ticket for you, and you'll go to Florida, but when you get there, go to the place that he'll tell you about. You'll have a place to stay and meals.

Kathy sent an e-mail to her brother John with information to give to David about picking up money at Western Union, about a possible biological family member in the area, David's Social Security number, a list of cheap places to stay, and a free (to him) place to stay: Covenant House.

John, ever light of heart, sent this e-mail to Kathy:

> Dear Kath: So, Dr. Livingston is off. He will need some summer duds when he gets there as he has mostly winter stuff. I have told him as soon as he gets a fixed address we will find some lighter stuff and overnight it. Remind Dave to find the local library where he can access the Internet, phone books, etc. I have enclosed a brief resource list from the area which you can give him over the phone if he has not lost his pencil and paper yet.
>
> You may be able to fax it to him at the Western Union Office in the bus depot.
>
> This should be quite interesting.
>
> All my love. JN

When John put David on the bus, that would be the last time the two saw each other. John would be dead of lung cancer in just a few years. But he had served David faithfully and with a creative bent.

Covenant House—a shelter for homeless kids—had a branch in Ft. Lauderdale (its main facility was in New York City). That's where we intended for him to land; Kathy had done all the work to make sure he could have a safe and supportive place.

Here was her e-mail communication to the shelter:

> I am hoping that our 17-year-old son has contacted you and that he may be at your facility. We gave him your address and phone number as a possible source of help in Fort Lauderdale. We offered a lot of alternatives when he got out of detox last Thursday, but David was adamant that he wants to be on his own, says he wants to go to work, and live away from our family where it is warm. He used to live on the streets in Fort Lauderdale with his biological dad and that's where he wanted to go. We believe he will probably need some assistance to achieve his goal. We would be happy to help with financial assistance (there is currently $100 waiting for him at the Western Union office at the bus station in Fort Lauderdale) or to contribute to your ministry as you are assisting him. Please feel free to contact us by e-mail or phone (616) _____ if we can help in any way. I told him that if he could find a room to rent, we would pay the first month's rent while he looks for a job and give him money for food. He has experience as a dishwasher in a restaurant. Our son had a very rough history from before we adopted him, but we have not abandoned him, despite what he may feel or say. . . . Thank you for caring about these kids.

Yours in Christ,

Kathy Neville (Dave's mom)

But, no, David did not immediately turn up at Covenant House. He met somebody on the bus—Jeff—and spent a couple weeks crashing with him.

Then he wanted us to front him $550 for a studio apartment so he could live with his new buddy. And Jeff was no longer welcome at Covenant House; he'd been kicked out before.

Only later did he link up with Covenant House. And, so, we made sure to underwrite David's keep, probably an unusual happenstance for that institution. Every two weeks Kathy sent $500. (And we continued to donate to their cause even after David left.)

David Faces Charges

David was in the 17-year-old grey area. But he had repeated run-ins with the law in Ft. Lauderdale, so they were watching for him. He was discharged from Covenant House for smoking in the facility, had been detained by the police, then moved to a shelter, where he slipped out through a window. The court was issuing a runaway pickup order for the police. And the county's Protective Service Department was alleging neglect and abandonment on our part as parents. David eventually moved back to Covenant House, but it was uneasy. At one point in April of 2002, Kathy made a note that his caseworker said David was getting ready to blow again.

Sooner, rather than later, he was picked up for shoplifting some booze. We didn't hear about it until nearly a month after it happened. As well, he discharged himself April 23 from Covenant House, but got a 14-day ticket so he could get food and use drop-in services. He was ordered to meet with a counselor twice a week for three months and perform 30 hours of community service. It was all too much for him, and his world was unraveling.

This is the notice we received at long last:

Court Mediation & Arbitration Program
North Regional Courthouse, Room 130
1600 W. Hillsboro Boulevard
Deerfield Beach, FL 33442
(954) 831-1291 Fax (954) 831-1296

CIRCUIT COURT OF THE
SEVENTEENTH JUDICIAL CIRCUIT
OF FLORIDA
IN AND FOR BROWARD COUNTY

South Regional Courthouse, Room 100B
3550 Hollywood Blvd.
Hollywood, FL 33021
(954) 831-0457 Fax (954) 831-0467

May 3, 2002

David Schock & Kathy Nevill (sic.)
545 Gidley Drive
Grand Haven, MI 49417

Re: David Schock

UC#: O2-4173 Teen Court No.: 7418
Date of Arrest: 04/03/2002

Charge: Retail Theft

Dear David Schock & Kathy Neville:

Your child has been referred to Court Mediation and Arbitration/Teen Court by the State Attorney's Office. As a result of this referral, your child is being considered for participation in the Teen Court Program. Please see the attached flyer which (sic.) explains Teen Court's operation.

In order to determine your child's appropriateness for the Teen Court Program, I am requesting that you contact me immediately to schedule an intake interview. In addition to this letter, an attempt was made to contact you by telephone. If I do not hear from you, the case will be referred back to the Juvenile Division of the State Attorney's Office for a filing decision. You must have attended an intake interview or completed the preliminary paperwork by 4:00 pm on 05/15/2002.

Sincerely yours,

G___ W_____, M.A., M.Ed.
Teen Court Counselor

Note: It is important that you arrive on time for your intake interview.

Encl.

It took a little while for the letter to reach us. When it did, Kathy again swung into action. First, she called, and then she wrote. She chronicled for the counselor every event, every move, every reason behind what David had chosen. She knew that otherwise we'd have been buried in the legal system.

To: G____ W_____, M. A., M. Ed., Teen Court Counselor FAX (954) 831-1296
From: Kathy Neville, J. D., Attorney and Mother
Re: David Schock

UC# 02-4173 Teen Court No.: 7418

Date of Arrest: 4-3-02

Charge: Retail Theft
Date: May 12, 2002

Your letter of May 3 regarding the above captioned matter arrived at our home on Saturday, May 11. I assume that the phone conversation I had with Maureen at your office constitutes "completed the preliminary paperwork," however, this letter constitutes a reiteration of my conversation with Maureen. I have provided my son David with a copy of your correspondence and asked him to contact you on Monday, May 13th. He checked into Covenant House in Fort Lauderdale today (Sunday, May 12) and has access to a phone. I believe there is a very low probability that he will actually show up for your program, however, I am most happy to have him participate. The most appropriate service for him at this time is Court-ordered substance abuse treatment. If the Court is willing to order him to be held in a locked juvenile detention facility, I am also willing to have him picked up and transported to an appropriate boarding school in another state by a bonded juvenile transport agency so that he can receive appropriate care. The details of his presence in Broward County follow.

These may be useful if he shows up for Teen Court and I would request that you forward this correspondence to the State if you refer him back there due to non-participation.

David completed a ten-day detox program in February; he refused to participate in a 90-day treatment program for substance abuse that we identified for him or to return to school. He also stated that he would hurt me if he was forced to return to our home, and stated clearly that he would be unable to control his rage, although he was unable to identify any specific reason he was angry, other than that we had rules and he feels that no rules should apply to him. He said his plan was to "disappear." In order to maintain contact and see if his stated plan to get a job panned out (David wanted to go to Fort Lauderdale to "get a job" where it is warm and where he lived prior to his adoption), we agreed that he could try this for 60 days. We offered multiple supports to assist David in the process of becoming independent once he got a job (help getting an apartment) and made arrangements for him to stay at an appropriate place until he found a job. To the best of my knowledge, David has yet to apply for even one job, even though he has now been in Florida for 90 days. Since about March 3, David has been saying he wants to enroll in Job Corps, but he has yet to finish the very simple paperwork required to complete the application, activities that would take about 2 hours. It appears that he prefers to commit retail theft; he also likes to claim that he was abandoned as an excuse to cover his substance abuse. The fact that this retail theft involved alcohol supports our contention that David abuses marijuana and alcohol and may be taking other substances. It appears to me that he is not ready to get a job and place to live, and we are prepared to get him the help he needs if you are willing to detain him. I believe David needs treatment. Court ordered treatment would be ideal, although I seriously doubt that you will order such treatment for retail theft. S___ R_____ of the Adoption Unit in Florida can describe the extraordinary efforts we have made to stabilize David and his two siblings.

Since the April 3 pick up, I have also had multiple discussions with S____ J____, an investigator from Broward County, regarding this case. I asked that David be picked up and locked up in a juvenile detention facility so that I could have a bonded juvenile transport agency (which I would pay for) take him to a boarding school in another state; at that time, I knew exactly where he was. She told me that you were unable to lock him up. She asked me to have our local police file a runaway report so she could. The local police refused to do so because of his age. Officer B_____ of the Grand Haven police called S____ J____ to inform her that the prosecutor in this county has decided that all 17-year-old juveniles will be treated for criminal purposes as adults; adults can't
have runaway reports because running away is a status offense. So we are stuck in a Catch-22. If, at any time, you wish to keep him in a locked detention center, I will facilitate the arrangements for transport and placement. Since the cost of transport is $2,500, I will do this when he is in a secure setting only. When S____ J_____ placed him in an open shelter, he went out the window and disappeared. I believe it would be very dangerous to fly him anywhere, even with police escort. He is not interested in going to boarding school. If you find him between May 26th and June 9th, I will be away on vacation. But I will be happy to make arrangements when I get back.

If you wish to ask additional questions or have other paperwork completed, please feel free to call me at -------- and leave a phone number and full name so that I can return your call. We remain strongly committed to our son; we have been through similar problems involving the juvenile justice system, the court, and the mental-health system in Michigan with both of David's biological siblings (who we also adopted) and are well known to all these agencies locally. David's siblings are both now sober, stable, happy, connected to us, and doing very well after doing time. It remains our hope that we will be able to achieve a similar outcome with David. One powerful incentive for change in the children has been our work with and the ability of the juvenile justice system to provide consequences for criminal behavior. We stand prepared to work with you to achieve a similar outcome for David.

Sincerely,

Kathy Neville

As she noted in her letter to the court, she wrote to David, too:

> May 13, 2002
> David—
>
> I faxed your letter from the Teen Court to Covenant House yesterday. I also called and told them you were aware that you needed to contact them.
>
> Up to you now.
>
> Jung Yi called me yesterday after I talked with you. She is very happy with her husband, her life, and with her new puppy, Roxie, which her husband bought her as a surprise for her birthday in April. She asked me to tell you that her life is very good and she hopes that someday yours will be, too.
>
> Although it was very hard for her because she loves you, she talked it over with her husband, and they asked me not to give you her telephone number at this time. Both Jung Yi and her husband are aware of the lifestyle you have been choosing the past two years and know what that is like since they had the same problems with alcohol and substances as teenagers. She does understand, and all of us continue to believe that you can get and stay sober if and when you decide you are willing to take a commitment to do so. They wanted me to tell you that they would like to hear from you after you get your life straightened out. By this, they mean that they would like to hear from you when you have shown an extended period of being off alcohol and substances, and are showing responsibility by working enough to support yourself for at least a few months. She says she has had enough trouble with people who are using to last a lifetime, and she doesn't want any more of that in her life. She also mentioned that what she had to do was put the past with your biological dad behind her and make a decision that she wanted a different life than he had. It wasn't easy at the beginning, but it got easier and really paid off for her. You can choose that future, too, if you decide to.
>
> We can talk about this again when you successfully complete the 28-day program at Covenant House and have been working for a while. Hope you have a good week. I'll keep you posted on your brother and sister's doings.
>
> Love, Mom

David Leaves Ft. Lauderdale

David decided that Ft. Lauderdale was not his final destination. Kathy had been in contact with Brother Fountain at Bethel Academy and several other possible boarding schools. David decided that he would go to Bethel in little Lucedale, MS, a world away from the streets of Ft. Lauderdale. Kathy recalled receiving a phone call from him saying that he wanted to leave, needed to leave.

Because David was older, he wouldn't fit in with the students in the boy's dorm, but Brother Fountain said he could find a place for him. He'd work with him. And so he was enrolled in the program.

Initially, we were going to have him transported by a bonded transport service, but instead he simply got on a bus. And he got off the bus at the right stop. He was met in Mobile on May 19, 2002 by Tommy from Bethel.

. . . Meanwhile in Broward County

The court—even knowing that David was then in Mississippi—decided to proceed on the matter to declare David a delinquent child. And we got the notice of case 02-4173 DL, before Judge Robert Collins:

> IN THE NAME AND BY THE AUTHORITY OF THE STATE OF FLORIDA:
>
> COMES NOW the State Attorney of the Seventeenth Judicial Circuit of Florida, in and for the County of Broward, by his undersigned duly authorized Assistant State Attorney, and petitions the Court for an adjudication of Delinquency as to the above-named Child/Children, and would show as follows:
> 1. This Court has jurisdiction of this cause as a juvenile case, in that:
> (a) the Child is under the age of eighteen (18) years, or was under such age at the time of the commission 0f the act(s) of delinquency set forth herein below;
> (b) the Child lives in, is domiciled in, or was found in Broward County, Florida; and
> (c) the Child is a delinquent child by virtue of the violation(s) of law as set forth herein below.
> 2. The Child is a delinquent child within the meaning of Chapter 985, Florida Statues, in that:
>
> DAVID SCHOCK on the 3rd day of APRIL A.D. 2002 in the County and State aforesaid did then and there unlawfully and knowingly obtain or use, or endeavor to obtain or use, the property of HUT LIQUOR STOR, to-wit: TRIPLE SEC MIXTURE, of the value of less than one-hundred dollars ($100.00) with the intent to either temporarily or permanently deprive HUT LIQUOR STORE of a right to the property or a benefit thereof, contrary to F.S. 812.014(1)(a) and F.S. 812.014(3)(a). SECOND DEGREE MISDEMEANOR, PETIT THEFT.

The petition went on to identify Kathy Neville as the parent and gave our address. I don't know why I wasn't listed, too, but it certainly kept things simpler. But there was a little more:

> WHEREFORE, Petitioner prays that the above-named Child/Children be adjudicated a Delinquent Child according to law.

MICHAEL J. SATZ
State Attorney
By: Martin W. Murphy
Assistant State Attorney FL Bar # 312991

And the whole thing was dated June 4th, 2002.

A subsequent notice dated June 6th from the court informed us that there was an arraignment hearing set for July 11th in the Broward County Courthouse. "The parent(s) or custodian are required to produce the child at the said time and place, unless the child is in detention or shelter care at said time."

The penalty if we didn't produce said child at 8:45 a.m. on July 11th? Contempt of court.

Kathy knew it was necessary to hire an attorney. She sought out one who had been recommended by an attorney who worked with Shepherd Care Ministries, the agency that had held the children in its care before they came to us. As a part of her letter to Mr. Diamond Kathy wrote:

> We have maintained a strong commitment to the children and the other two siblings are currently doing well after many, many problems. We remain hopeful that a positive outcome is also in David's future. David is diagnosed as having ADHD and conduct disorder and has had lots of therapy; a substance abuse evaluation early this year indicated that he is in the early stages of alcoholism. He voluntarily entered a treatment program at the Bethel Baptist Boys Academy in Lucedale, Mississippi, on May 20th; I am praying that we will not need to have him return to Fort Lauderdale on this case because it is likely to lead to renewed drug use and a return to the street.
>
> David has been charged with shoplifting Triple Sec in Broward County, his first charged criminal offense as far as I know. David is willing to admit responsibility for this charge. We would like to dispose of this matter as quickly and cheaply as possible without appearing (we live in Michigan). If necessary, we are requesting that our attorney appear on our behalf (and our son's) at the Arraignment to enter an appropriate guilty plea. Although I am licensed as an attorney in Michigan, I have not practiced criminal law for many years . . . and have no idea about the requirements for juveniles in Florida. We will be happy to sign any required waivers. Since David is 17, he is considered an adult in Michigan for legal purposes (based on decision made by the County Prosecutor here) and there is little we can do legally; they wouldn't even accept a runaway report when we were trying to have him transported from Florida for treatment. I would like to briefly explain how he came to Broward County. . . .

And then she included much of the information that she had shared with the Teen Counselor in the diversion program. She added:

> Following David's intake contact with Teen Court (when he found out he would have to do 30 hours of community service), he requested that we place him in boarding school and we made the arrangements. He did not complete the Teen Court intake. David voluntarily entered Bethel Baptist Boys Academy . . . on May 20th. [. . .] This is a faith-based, Marine boot camp type program where he can work on his GED (he has yet to finish the ninth grade), learn construction trades, and address his alcohol and drug problems. It is very highly structured with daily Physical Training. We pay $1,500 per month for this program and believe it is appropriate to David's treatment need. We anticipate that he will remain there until he is 18.
>
> During David's stay in Florida, we worked actively with C____ F_____, a case manager at Covenant House, S____ F_____, an investigator for the Broward County Police, and M_____ H_____ of the Teen Court to achieve this result. All of them can vouch for the care, support, and work we did to help David to decide to seek treatment.
>
> Your assistance in this matter would be greatly appreciated.

Mr. Diamond came through. He filed a request and the court appointed him to represent David and us in court. The guilty plea was entered June 24th.

In an ironic twist, the court the next day sent out a "Mandatory Subpoena" for Kathy to appear at a trial scheduled for 8:45 a.m. July 3, 2002 in room 5840 of the Broward County Courthouse, 201 S.E. Sixth Street, Fort Lauderdale. The subpoena—a standby subpoena—made it clear that the matter may already have been resolved by a plea, and so Kathy was to make the call to either the witness liaison or the State Attorney's office. I'm sure that was a call she made.

There probably were court costs and restitution. Certainly there were attorney and legal fees, but David stayed in Lucedale. And we stayed in Michigan. And we were grateful. Kathy and I had long known that our children—as long as they were under 18—could involve us in untold legal matters. Overall I think we were fortunate there weren't more. If it hadn't been for Kathy and her knowledge of law we'd have been in a pickle. What about other families who don't have access to a mom who was also a lawyer? I wonder.

And I wonder about what David was going through at this time. Oh, there was no question that we were not pleased by his conduct and choices. Overall, he was still headed for trouble, and no matter how much we loved him, there wasn't going to be a whole lot we could do if he moved into more criminal behavior. For now we had him in a relatively safe place; there would be someone to watch him every minute of every day.

David Works His Program

Brother Fountain would keep him in the program until he was 18. For his part, David said he was looking forward to learning to box, a specialty of the school. His enthusiasm lasted a few rounds when he fought some tough guys two days after his arrival; David did not like pain.

When he reached his 18th birthday, Brother Fountain lined up a job working with a local fencing company, Havard's Fence Building. In time David would come to live in a little house Mr. Havard found for him in the middle of his neighbor's back pasture. Beef cattle would come up and nuzzle against his window screens he told me in a phone call. Later, I was to see it for myself.

Daniel Does Well . . . For a Time

As far as Daniel's progress, he seemed to thrive on the discipline and leadership that also appealed to his intellect. Brother Gerhardt—well educated and well versed—talked with him, reasoned with him, and worked with him to develop as a leader among students.

I wrote him several letters. The first was from June 17, 2002:

> Dear Daniel:
>
> I was glad that we could talk with you on Friday. It's very pleasant to hear what you're doing and planning. The idea that you are really applying yourself to your studies is great. I believe you can make as much progress as you set your mind to. There is no lack of ability on your part. It's determination, learning how to work effectively, and the support to get it all done.
>
> I had a rehearsal yesterday at church. It seems that Lynn Middlebrook is putting together a brass choir for worship and I think it's a great idea. Our first meeting resulted in a lot of classical playing and some hymns. We sound pretty good. Intonation is always a tricky bit.
>
> In addition to working on a documentary this summer, I've been playing in the mud . . . working in the yard. The little strip of grass between the sidewalk and the street has been receiving my attentions of late. There was too much dirt there, so I took out all the old sod, took out ten wheelbarrows of dirt, and now am ready to plant a tree and then seed the grass. It's been a lot of fun.
>
> We bought a new lawn mower last summer . . . again, an engine to turn the blade but the rest is all push. I'm wondering if I might not be getting a little old for that! I'm tired when I'm done.
>
> Mom is well recovered from her cold and we're all fine . . . Jack, Lenny, Archie, and Penny.[7]

---

[7] The dog and three cats.

I send my love.

Dad

P.S. Did Pastor Gerhardt okay your writing to Brother Fountain to thank him? We talked with him recently and conveyed your gratitude and all the good news about your progress. He is very happy for all that God is doing in your life. It's true, son: you are moving from strength to strength. I pray you all the success in the world.

Daniel seemed to be applying himself and had found in Brother Gerhardt a model of moral rectitude and civility. I wrote him again November 2, 2002:

Dear Daniel:

I am so pleased that your school work is coming along so well. Completing Paces at this rate may well put you on track for your desired graduation time. That really WOULD be wonderful . . . getting caught up and on track.

I am glad to hear that Brother Gerhardt and his family were able to get away for a vacation. There's a lot of work to make that school go. Glad to hear, as well, that two new boys are scheduled to arrive and join in the program.

Our semester at college is more than halfway complete, but it seems to grow busier and busier. I have to go down to my office later today to grade a very tall stack of papers. I finished teaching a half-term class of Introduction to Mass Communication and now have to grade 35 final exams, plus twenty term papers that are being resubmitted . . . all that plus the regular grading that comes in every week . . . quizzes and assignments. Well, it will be finished soon enough and there's always plenty of work. I hate to feel like I'm falling behind. Next week, too, my broadcast journalism students are doing a live three-hour television show on election-night coverage. It's really going to be some work on their part. My students this semester are some of the best I've ever encountered and it's a real thrill to see them tackling hard issues.

I'm still playing lots of music. Right after I get up each morning I go down to feed Lenny and I sit down and practice for the first ten minutes . . . long tones and slurs. That way even if the day goes long and I don't find my way to the horn again, I've completed the minimum I need in order to keep playing. I have several concerts upcoming, but none in the next couple of weeks. How goes your singing? Are you practicing the materials Mr. Seise wanted you to work on?[8] Practice really does make a difference and the idea that you might be able to share your gift with others

---

[8] Daniel had taken some voice lessons with a local performer/teacher, Carlos Seise, a gifted tenor. Seise said that he thought Daniel had some natural ability and would take him as a pupil—even remotely and occasionally—IF Daniel would do the work.

and earn a living at the same time is pretty exciting to me. Of course, you're the guy who has to do the work!

Grandma is coming to visit today. We hope she'll be staying a month or so. She is such fun and really appreciates anything we do for her. I anticipate that we'll be taking her out to Russ' restaurant a time or two while she's here.

Jack and the cats are all just fine. We had a stray puppy show up last night and mom is working at finding the owner . . . this is a little dog who has been much loved so we'll try to get her back to where she belongs as fast as we can.[9]

I send you my love. It's cold here and we've actually had snow already . . . not much stayed on the ground, but it fell from the sky!

Love,

But not everyone liked the school. At one point the *St. Louis Post Dispatch* did an article, claiming Mountain Park was unregulated in any way, thought by many to be a hellhole.

The reporter called Kathy for comment, and she discussed the school:

> Kathy Neville, whose son attends Mountain Park, said she knows the school's methods may sound severe. But Neville, who does not share the school's fundamentalist faith, said she had tried everything to turn around her son, including professional therapy.
>
> Neville, of Grand Haven, Mich., is a lawyer and former social worker who says she has worked for years in jobs related to mental health.
>
> She won't discuss the specifics of her son's condition but says he needs an extraordinarily rigid environment, with hard rules and predictable routines. He also needs to be isolated from negative peer pressure, which is something state-run juvenile programs were unable to provide.
>
> "The kind of structure they have in their program is very consistent with good behavioral practice," she said.
>
> She and other parents also support the limits on communication. Neville said she knows her boy and is certain his correspondence is honest and candid. He recently

---

[9] The little dog never was claimed and became our beloved Gracie. I gave her an expanded first, middle, and last of Gracie Maybelle Wigglebutt, the which never ceased to entertain children on our regular evening walks. Gracie was the sweetest stray who'd ever come our way . . . part Lab, part Vizsla, maybe some beagle. We also had Lenny, a big cat who we found as a kitten in the weeds along a road where he'd been tossed. I don't know that Kathy much likes my description, but I have referred to our family as a family of strays . . . all of us.

was allowed to visit home and never uttered a bad word about the school, Neville said.[10]

But there is now a website for survivors of what they are calling cult education. And we later learned that a student had died there in 1986. There are both supporters and detractors.

Visiting David

Daniel was in the equivalent of his rising senior year at Mountain Park. On his summer break, I picked him up from the school the last day of May 2003, and we drove to Lucedale to visit David, something I remember as a long trip first through mountains and then flatlands. On the flat we were graced with the omnipresent scent of Confederate Jasmine or Carolina Jessamine. Mile after mile.

David's little house could be reached either by walking through the pasture or via a minimal two-track. Overhanging branches scratched the paint on the car in a few places.

David liked where he was living. Everything was tidy. His few dishes were washed. His bed was made.

We fit three of us in a two-seat BMW convertible. They didn't mind but I wondered if I might get stopped. With Michigan license plates any law enforcer looking at us probably figured it was just another crazy northerner.

We went out to eat barbeque, a specialty that shows up at gas stations in the rural South. The generous ribs were fall-off-the bone done and smoky rich. The best I've ever eaten. David and Daniel agreed. We made that gas station a regular destination for our few days there.

And we shopped at the new local Wal-Mart Supercenter. We talked with people who worked there and were visiting, some like us for the first time. That Wal-Mart had galvanized the town; Lucedale had become a regional shopping center. People were pouring into town like they hadn't done since the '30s and '40s.

We ate at several other sit-down restaurants, too, and talked and talked. David talked of his work installing fences. His boss, Joe Havard, was good to work for and the work was interesting; he worked hard but was fairly paid. He was studying for his GED with Mr. Havard's support and encouragement. They would talk a lot, David said, about stuff. God, work, family.

---

[10] Matthew Franck. "Graduates are divided between survivors and supporters," St. Louis Post Dispatch, November 21, 2002. https://culteducation.com/group/1059-mountain-park-baptist-church-and-boarding-academy/14592-graduates-are-divided-between-survivors-and-supporters.html

He spent some of each week at Mr. Havard's home and with his family, most often for a meal. He'd been to their home for many dinners and celebrations. Even Easter. There is a picture of David on an Easter egg hunt with the little Havard grandchildren.

I could tell that Joe Havard was another of those presences who stand to relieve misery and darkness. I would later learn that after decades in the shipyards, Joe had started his business, and made it a point to reach out to young people who were having a hard time. David was one of many. He treated each one of them with dignity and respect.

David, shy when talking about important things, lit up when he talked about him. It may have been David at his best; I think it was. He was leading his own life and the possibilities unrolled before him like sod over tilled and leveled earth. His fences were strong and straight. He was learning and living what he learned. I urged him to stay with Mr. Havard and take in all he could.

Daniel and David at David's house during our visit in Lucedale, MS. The little house in the middle of the pasture is in the background.

When it was time to go, Daniel and I loaded up the car for a trip north. We were going north and east to tour Crown College in Powell, Tennessee, just north of Knoxville. Crown College, a Baptist bastion, was high on Brother Gerhardt's list for Daniel's continued spiritual growth. After the tour we were headed for Grand Haven for the rest of Daniel's summer break; it would be his first time home since he left for Bethel Boys'. The brothers said their goodbyes and I left David with a hug, telling him I loved him, and my hope that things would continue.

They wouldn't.

80

A Dark Intervention

How did it happen that their biological mother resurfaced? I can't remember, but there must have been a phone call. It may have come from JungYi who had heard through her Knoxville family that her mother, Yi-Huicha McNutt, was living in Chicago and wanted her children. We talked with JungYi about her right as an adult to have contact with her biological mother if she wished. But we judged that the boys, because they were under 18, needed to be shielded. We asked JungYi to not relay the information to the boys. She didn't. We knew it wouldn't last, not because JungYi would act against what we had asked of her, but because of the nature of the information. Katy and I believed that when they reached 18 the children should be able to decide for themselves what they wanted to do, go where they wanted to go, affiliate with whom they wished. Our goal had been to keep them alive until 25 (and beyond), at which age we thought we might be able to enter into the adult-adult relationships that we had so valued with some of the members of our own families.

Either the children's biological mother flew out to visit JungYi, or she paid for a ticket for our daughter to fly to Chicago. I don't remember. I do remember hearing from her that she had been overwhelmed with gifts and money. There was a cell phone, for instance, and her mother was paying for all the expenses.

The luster quickly faded. There were demands, and her mother wasn't well. If JungYi didn't answer when her biological mother called, she would be punished; what kind of a daughter was she who wouldn't honor her mother? There were regular tongue-lashings.

We hoped that JungYi could withstand it all, and we encouraged her, never made demands, didn't try to force a choice in allegiance. We understood the power of wanting a relationship with a parent, no matter how unlikely that it would be a good relationship. We could see nothing to befit our daughter or our sons, but at a certain point, we knew that the matter would have to rest with them.

I remember telling David and Daniel separately about their mother wanting to reach out to them. But the telling had to have been proximal; they could not have kept this news from each other.

They had questions, mostly about how they could speak with her.

It didn't take long for Yi-Huicha to drive down to Lucedale with her husband, Appa, gather up David, fly with him to California to visit JungYi and then take him to live with her in Chicago. He left a safe place and entered a world that would consume him.

He suddenly had a lot of stuff, but it came with the price of unquestioned filial devotion, even in the face of the most outrageous demands. David reported that it wasn't much fun, eventually telling us that his mother was mentally ill. It fit. Still, he found he could not make a clean break of it. He would leave her household and come back, depending on his finances.

And those finances would depend on whether he was drinking. So would much else. When he was sober, he was a good employee. When he was sober, he was a good son to us, too, calling and talking, making jokes.

Sometime in all that he found Maggie. Eventually he moved from his mother's house to her household. She stuck with him through a lot. But when he was drinking, she and her mother had the good sense to put him out, even if temporarily. And at those times, he bounced, homeless.

Mountain Park Closes, Daniel Comes Home

In the end Daniel would have a hand in closing the school with something he did . . . we still don't know what, but I think it involved him preventing another student from using a bathroom for a long time, some kind of hazing. After parental complaints and an official investigation, the school closed before it could be shut down.

Daniel came home to Grand Haven with some sort of high-school equivalency. With Brother Gerhardt's help, he had been accepted to Crown College. He spent the summer working at the local Burger King. He made a visit to his mother in Chicago and came back with gifts, clothes, a laptop. She made the offer of a cell phone, and as with JungYi she'd pay the charges. We told him that even though his mother might want him to have a phone, we didn't. We didn't want it in our house. Kathy and I saw it as an intrusion, a direct line, an umbilicus to a voice we heard as damaging. Our position was that if he wanted the phone he'd need to live elsewhere.

One bright spot was his involvement with a local Baptist congregation. He managed to reach out to his former daycare provider and her husband, Laurie and Howie. He brought them into the fold, what he called soul-winning.

For all that, Daniel came back into the house and started behaving pretty much the same way he had when he was 12 . . . in opposition to any authority. If we asked him to not smoke in the house, the house would be layered when we walked in the door. His laundry? Couldn't be bothered. Clean up after himself? No. Alcohol. Drugs. Worst, when I wasn't around, he, too, was threatening to Kathy.

Late nights he'd head out the door, claiming he was going running. What he was doing was meeting friend for drugs. He'd come back goofed.

One morning Kathy followed Daniel out the door. He went around the side of a neighbor's house and pulled out a cell phone.

We confronted him. Well, his mother had mailed it to Laurie and Howie, and he picked it up from them.

We told him we didn't want it in the house. What we wanted did not matter.

"It's like Satan living in the house," Kathy said. I did not disagree. Still, with only three weeks left, our goal was to make it through the summer, deliver him to Crown College and then see what might develop. There was always the hope the maturation process might engage.

Our communication with the college stipulated that we would pay for room, board, and tuition ONLY. The rest was to be on Daniel. This was why he had worked over the summer.

August 27, 2004, I was back teaching at Hope College when Kathy drove Daniel to Crown. It was, she said, a long, unpleasant drive. Daniel knew that this first semester was on us. The rest was in doubt.

When Kathy returned, we talked at length. For all his appearance before those outside the house of following a right path, we knew it wasn't genuine. So I sent another letter in late September, alerting him that we were not going to fund a second semester. We wanted to give him time to make plans.

> Dear Dan:
>
> I hope you are enjoying college and that you're learning something that will profit you and others. I have not written before, not e-mailed, not called because I've been thinking over what has passed between us and what is ahead.
>
> What has passed between us is this: when you came home after being asked to leave Mountain Park we set the ground rules: no drugs, no alcohol, and nothing but the truth. You know as well as I do the result.
>
> We further set up another stipulation: no cell phone from your mother in our house. And you know the result of that.
>
> Did you wonder that I didn't wake you on your last day home? I was pretty angry then and I am angry now. Oh, we knew; it was no secret. We'd been zeroed in on both the drugs and the phone for some time. Your disrespect for us, our house, our rules is a guarantee that we're not offering you a place to live again. It's not going to happen.
>
> The question in my mind is what's going to happen to any further schooling. That, too, was *quid pro quo*. I know that your mother has talked of giving you a car and paying for your insurance. I suggest that in addition—or instead—she pay for your education; it's a better investment if she has to make a choice.
>
> Kathy has suggested that we phrase it this way: we're retiring from parenting. That's one way to put it. Another is that after careful and prayerful consideration we've decided that there is no reason why we would ever volunteer for the kind of

> treatment you dished out in our home this summer. We like having our home back, we like not having to wonder what you were going to do next.
>
> We're pretty sure you'll do well; you've been most successful are getting what you want, no matter the cost to other people. And those other people may not be bothered at the basic deceit involved; they are not likely to be offended if you lie or tell less than the full truth. But we are.
>
> So, what's ahead? Well, we think it's great if you can make plans for Thanksgiving and you may want to call your mother for your Christmas break and for your next semester's tuition and fees. Or you may want to do something else. But you're not going to do it here.
>
> We love you still. But we find—on the whole—you have not yet changed into the man that we believe God has called you to be. And your actions have spoken louder than any words you might have uttered.

And then we got a bill from the college for $300 to cover the cost of a "choir outfit" for a trip to New York. We contacted the college and let them know that the Jones of New York suit, the shirt, and the tie and the trip should be on Daniel per our agreement.

His first semester grades came. Overall not bad, but there was a "D" in History of Civilization I. There were some very good grades, too. "A"s in English Grammar, College Choir, Old Testament Survey, and Vocal Techniques. And a "A+" in Personal Evangelism.

But we remained firm that we were not going to pay for his going back to Crown.

Somehow, he gathered enough money to start the semester from the local Baptist congregation and perhaps from his mother.

Because we believed that people always can change and even very suddenly follow a better path, whatever else happened we kept the lines of communication open.

Daniel said he liked the school, but his laptop—the one his mother had given him—had been stolen. He'd need another one. As things turned out, it hadn't been stolen; he'd given it to a classmate, somehow sure of its replacement from his biological mother. I don't think that happened, and he had to limp along using a school computer for his assignments.

He finished his second semester, owing more than a thousand dollars. He spent the summer at the college, working on the maintenance crew to earn money to pay his debt and to get ahead on the next semester.

The next semester would not arrive. According to his sister, he was kicked out of the program because he got caught smoking a cigarette.

The program was pretty strict, and we knew it could be so.

"Of all the schools, why would he attend the one where he's not allowed to smoke . . . if that's what he really wants to do?" Kathy asked.

But we thought there might have been another reason or reasons for his being sent down.

Then he moved to Chicago to be with his mother. He would remain there.

Daniel came back for a visit, probably in the summer of 2006. I met him at a local restaurant. When he put his hands on the table, I took a good look. There were two small tattoo marks on the web of his right thumb and forefingers.

"I was just goofing around getting a tattoo," he said.

I knew better and let him know. Those were the start of a tat for those who have done time in prison. When completed, there would be five dots in all . . . a square with one dot in the center. I asked him if he was running with the Latin Kings, a gang notorious in our local market and in Chicago.

No, nothing like that, he said.

"I was born at night, but it wasn't last night," I told him. "I know Latin Kings. And if you're with them you want to think about it; it doesn't end well for you."

But David had been hanging with them, Daniel said, attempting to deflect attention away from himself. Though half Korean, both boys could pass for Latin. When he had been in the South, David had said he often had been called a "Beaner," derogatory slang for a Mexican.

Daniel said David's nickname then was "Chino Dollaa." Chinese Dollar? An acknowledgement by the gang that its members viewed him as Asian, even Chinese.

David later told us Daniel was more of a wannabe. And while he had perhaps been in jail, he never had been in prison. But he was fitting himself for the role. Daniel returned to Chicago.

During the next year we kept in touch with all three children by telephone.

By the next summer, David was doing better and had achieved regular sobriety. He had been enrolled in an introductory firefighting course—Intro to Fire Science—at the College of DuPage and he liked his instructor. He had completed one semester and was anticipating another. Maybe this was something he could do, he said. And he had a paying job behind a deli counter in a grocery store. He was good at his work and got along well with his colleagues.

When he asked if he could come and visit with Maggie, we assented.

Friday, August 10, 2007

We were entirely taken with Maggie, young, hopeful and—for David—very helpful. We talked, ate, David and I played a few trumpet duets. It was evident that his musical sense had matured; he could put four in a bar. And he was practicing guitar regularly.

It was a very good day. When they climbed back in the car for the three-hour trip to Chicago, I knew that I would miss them. It would be the last time I saw my son alive.

David, during his final visit to the house.

Daniel Returns

Suddenly that fall Daniel was back in Grand Haven, first staying with Laurie and Howie and then moving into an apartment with several other young men from the church. We figured he was on the run, either from the gang or the law, or maybe both. For a time he was able to hold together the appearance of change. We would meet for lunch or dinner. Sometimes he would accompany me to a concert I was playing downtown. I enjoyed spending time with him and hoped and wished that he would develop the integrity that I believed could be there.

Was he working for a time or just "looking?" I think there were problems with him paying his rent. I know I helped out a time or two. But soon he was no longer living there, and he dropped out of contact.

He met a young and impressionable girl, Ashley, and convinced her and her family that he should move in. Daniel is both good looking and had the veneer of middle-class manners, something we worked so hard to give him and his brother and sister. Now it was paying off for him in ways we never anticipated.

He stopped by to introduce the girlfriend and to show off his car, a rolling death trap. Daniel didn't know much about cars. For his Christmas gift, I paid for new brakes, installed by a neighbor of his in the trailer park.

We learned that Daniel had started to flash money and fine items, brand-name leather wallets. We knew his sporadic work wasn't bringing that in.

It took a while for the Sheriff's Department to catch up to him, but he was arrested January 29, 2008, and then arraigned Feb. 6. Daniel had been burgling garages and selling what he'd stolen, and doing smash and grabs from parked cars. Very often women would leave their purses visible in their cars, lock the doors, and go off to enjoy the local scenery. A windshield is no match for a hammer. Daniel was quick. And he'd grab cash and credit cards, take the cards to a local mall and buy things (all the while under video scrutiny), then toss the cards on the way out the door. The offense he was charged with occurred October 30, 2007.

I have gone back through my daily diary to see the days when I drove to the Muskegon County Jail to visit him. There are probably ten visits in all on Thursday mornings, usually at 10 a.m.

At one point Daniel asked about me furnishing bail. He knew I always had said that were he arrested there would be no bail. In the first place, if he'd done the crime, he should plead to it and save everybody a lot of hassle. In the second, as long as he was in jail and guilty, he was already serving his time . . . days that would be counted as already served when it came time for sentencing.

Dan—as he then called himself—tried to convince us that he could serve a shorter term—less than a year—in the county jail if he was furnished with a private attorney. He could stay out of prison. Maybe.

My experience has taught me that public defenders usually are attorneys who are as well or better experienced in the law than high-priced call-ins. We declined his invitation to fund the enterprise.

He pled in May and was sentenced to a term of not more than 18 months, a Cobbs Plea. And off he went, initially to the Michigan State Prison in Jackson, the first place all prisoners land. After an initial few months there, he was transferred to the Richard A. Handlon Correctional Facility at Ionia where he served out his time. I have letters to and from Daniel through that period.

Here's one I sent to him from June 6, 2008:

> Dear Dan:
>
> You have been in my thoughts and prayers. I can only imagine prison life as not very pleasant. Still, there is routine, order, people and opportunities for spiritual and emotional growth. That certainly doesn't make it easy, though. So I hope you are doing well, are staying out of trouble.
>
> You know how I said I'd send on little things from time to time? Here's one from Dec. 21, 1998:
>
>> Daniel—you are to copy this 1,000 times . . . by hand.
>>
>> Lie not to one another, seeing that ye have put off the old man with his deeds; and have put on the new man which is renewed in knowledge after the image of him that created him. Colossians 3: 9-10.
>
> That's just in case you've been wondering how long all this has been going on. Long time. I remember you writing this out during the space of a couple of days. And this was AFTER we'd tried a hundred or so of some other verse for an earlier punishment. I remember we burnt the pages from this punishment in the fireplace. That wasn't the most fun Christmas.
>
> So, what does this have to do with your life now? A lot or a little, and it depends entirely on you and what you decide to DO. You know my prayer: that you become a new man in Christ and lead a blameless life, neither lying nor stealing, and being honest with everybody including yourself. But that takes a real concern for others, for their wellbeing, sometimes even at the expense of your own. The question then becomes "How do you care for others?" Part of it is developing the ability to see that others suffer, too. When you were in jail one of the things I talked about was the fright you engendered in the women whose money and credit

cards you stole. You said you didn't think about the fear they might have to live with . . . somebody who had their most precious documents and who knew where they lived, how they lived, who would not hesitate to break a car window to get what he wanted. How do you think they felt at night? Did they worry that someone was coming to hurt them?

There are people out there who would enjoy others fearing them. I can't begin to tell you how sick that is. But you've seen it as a child. Who in his right mind would want to hurt a child, would want to inflict suffering? And I suppose it's natural to treat others as we've been treated. That applies, mind you, if there is no choice made to behave in an alternate fashion. And that's where faith steps in. Just because it was done to you does not mean you have to pass it on. You can choose to take a different path, to lead a different life. But you have to choose it.

Believe me, if I didn't think you could, I wouldn't be writing this letter; it would be a waste of time. But I DO believe that you can change, and I pray—every day—that you will make a new choice. But I know it's not something you can just say . . . you have to live it and that takes time to show a new choice.

I hope there are opportunities to read and study and that you will have the chance to keep on learning, even if not in a formal setting. I'm sure you're getting an education from observing those around you. I pray you are safe.

Love,

Dad

Letters, yes. Visits . . . no. Well, just one. And that happened after trying to get on his visitor's list.

It took several trips to be allowed in to visit Daniel. On the first attempt something had happened within the prison and all visiting hours were denied. The next time I was successful, but visitors are required to go through quite a search process to be allowed inside. And I learned something that I wished I had known. The visiting room where I met with Daniel was walled with vending machines. Visitors usually come in with pockets stuffed with change. They feed the machines and the inmates get treats not usual in their commissary selections. I came with precious little change, not nearly enough. Kathy put $50 in Daniel's account every month. I put in extra at birthdays and Christmas. But that day would have been better with bulging pockets of quarters.

David Comes to a Shelter

David really wasn't doing well. After his educational efforts at the community college, he started spiraling. He had resumed drinking, and for an alcoholic any is way too much. Somehow, he got himself to California to visit and stay with JungYi and Curtis. But things were crazy with him there: he was drinking, drugging, stealing, creating chaos. The low point was an attempted suicide. David, who as a little boy and young man hated needles and all pain, had cut his wrists and bled all over the carpet in the master bedroom. Curtis made it clear that he wanted David to leave, and soon.

For his part, David knew he was scraping bottom and wanted to get things back on track. He wanted to come back to Grand Haven. Having him live in the house was not going to happen, but we found space for him at the Holland Rescue Mission. He came in on a bus from southern California. I met him September 19th, 2008, and I took him to settle in. The rescue mission is noted for its supportive treatment program and care of individuals who have hit bottom. But David would have to remain sober if he wanted to keep his berth. I would come back the next day and take him out for lunch.

I thought that as a part of the struggle, it might be helpful if I drove down to him regularly.

In an Oct. 4 letter to Daniel, Kathy wrote:

> David is doing well so far. He is staying at the Holland Rescue Mission, completed his evaluation, and was invited to stay in a smaller dorm. It's a very nice place with a big emphasis on helping people get a new life set up if they are motivated. He started a full time job doing temp work at a factory three of four days ago (working afternoons). He rides a bicycle for a half hour each way to get to work and back. This shows his motivation. He hopes to be hired in after 90 days because it pays well. This is a good start. Dad met him for coffee twice this week. He will be budgeting and saving toward getting his own apartment. As he says, he is a good worker unless he starts drinking and then he doesn't care. Dad told him that this is a really nice place compared to the other options. If he leaves or gets kicked out, he would be at one of those "other options" and can't return to the place in Holland for 60 days. So he is taking advantage of this right now. Dad said he realized from living there that he really doesn't have any problems compared to a lot of the people there. What a great insight!

For his part, Daniel was earning his GED; he couldn't prove that attainment because of the closure of the school. There had been charges pending in Chicago, but because of his incarceration in Michigan they were being dropped. Otherwise, as soon as his bid was up in Michigan he could have been headed for trial in Illinois. As it was Daniel would need to stay in Michigan through his probation.

David and I would meet frequently. And he would complain: about the other residents, the theft of his cell-phone charger, the arguments. I took him to buy a new charger. I remember coffees, snacks, and one noon we had a lunch at Culver's.

In another letter to Daniel, Kathy noted that David was still with the program almost a month out:

> Dad had lunch with David the other day. He is still working and living at the Holland Rescue Mission as of then. Although it isn't his first choice of where he would like to live, he understands that it takes some time to start over and save

enough money to get your own place to live. When you get out of prison, you may be facing the same situation of starting over. David seems to be maturing in understanding that he is an adult man now—staying positive and upbeat even though he may not love everything about his current situation. He is working toward the right goal for an adult man of getting his own place to live. His paycheck goes into an account at the Mission for this purpose. The upside of having and paying for your own place in your 20s is that you have freedom to live your own lifestyle (smoking, friends, hours awake, noise level, and so on). Once people get to be 20-something, they have very individual ideas about what the rules in their home should be. I told him what I told you one night when you called at 11 pm and said you were "homeless": as long as you are living for free on someone's couch, you are only one argument away from being homeless. Once you are paying rent, you know you have a place and until when. Living with other adults who are setting the rules and not supporting yourself keeps you feeling like a child instead of being an adult with your own plans, dreams, and hobbies, [someone] who is in charge of your own life. Dad and I know this attitude about being responsible for yourself as men is best for both of you at this point in your life. It is also best for us. Our home is a quiet sanctuary, and we like it that way. We are past the time in our lives when we choose to have drama and conflict in our home.

Love, Mom

As Kathy said when I asked her for this letter: "I love my children, but I told them what I thought." It was the best thing she could do for them. And they really had no idea that this educated, trained and skilled social worker, attorney, and Master of Divinity graduate had their backs and worked ceaselessly for their benefit. Ceaselessly and mindfully.

And both Kathy and I knew the damage that alcohol and drugs could do to families. We'd each seen it, she more closely than I.

Our correspondence with Daniel was ongoing. Here's a letter from me to him from October 21, 2008:

Dear Dan:

I pray you are well. It's been good to read your letters. The one in front of me is probably the third that's come in between my letters to you.

[. . .]

You know, you wrote about perhaps being a psychologist and working with kids who are having trouble. That could happen, I think. It would take a lot of study and a whole lot of work and luck but I believe you could do that if you wanted just that more than anything else in the world. You'd certainly understand what it felt like to them and what they were going through. And by that time you'd have the skills to understand yourself well, too.

David thinks he's headed for the Army. As far as I know he's signed up and has to get some clearances and his gang tat obscured. I'll be seeing him tomorrow afternoon and having lunch with him. He's been working for a temp service and even though one assignment ended he said he's got great recommendations so he's not likely to be out of work for long. I'll know more after I see him and we chat. I'm going to take down some labels so that he can easily write to you. He says he'd like to touch base with you.

The weather is getting much colder . . . no surprise there. We've had such a beautiful summer and fall and I guess the snow must be next. Okay. Oh, trick-and-treaters will be next, I'm guessing. I remember you guys out running for loot.

[. . .]

Love,

David B. Schock

As I wrote Daniel, David and I had made plans. I had invited him to come to a pow wow that was being held in Holland. It would be a chance for him to see a little something of a small but significant part of his heritage. I'd come and pick him up.

Instead, when I called him the day of the event to set up a time, he answered his phone and told me he couldn't come. A day later, I learned that he had returned to Chicago.

This is how Kathy informed Daniel of David's struggles:

> David returned to Chicago yesterday or the day before. I believe that someone he knows came to pick him up, then they went to Mt. Prospect and picked up the car from your Mom's house. Apparently David has returned to drinking. Your friends in Chicago will probably know more about where he will be living and what he is doing than we do or will.
>
> That's all the news for now. Study hard.
>
> Love, Mom

David had been in and out of homeless shelters as his drinking picked up. He had not called in some time; he was more apt to call when things were going well. So when I got a phone call from him on a Friday late in the year, I was at first hopeful.

Friday, Dec. 5, 2008

"Hi, Dad. This is your son. I won't be coming home for a visit any time soon."

Why was that?

"I got arrested yesterday."

What for?

"Robbing a bank."

Are you all right?

"Yeah, it was really dumb."

Was anybody else hurt?

"No."

Did you use a gun?

"No."

Did you threaten anybody?

"Um . . . ."

And where are you now?

"I'm here with an FBI agent. He's letting me use his phone."

You need to thank him; he doesn't have to do that.

Aside: "My dad says I need to thank you. Thank you."

Were you drinking?

"Ummmm, yeah."

Are they taking you for an arraignment?

"I don't know. I guess I'm going to jail."

I told him I loved him and that I was very glad no one was hurt. That was the critical element. He told me he loved us both and he was sorry.

According to the Chicago area *Daily Herald* of December 5, 2008:

> **Man arrested in Arlington Heights bank robbery.**
>
> By Frieda Gad
>
> Arlington Heights police have arrested a man in connection with the robbery Thursday afternoon of the Chase Bank at 43 E. Golf Road in Arlington Heights.
>
> David Schock, 23, who is apparently homeless with no known address, was charged Friday with one count of bank robbery, a felony offense. He will be held without bond until his next appearance Wednesday at U.S. District Court in Chicago.
>
> Bank staff gave police a description of the robber and within about a half-hour of the 2:30 p.m. robbery, a plainclothes officer found a suspect about a half-mile from the bank, Cmdr. Kenneth Galinski said Friday. The man was turned over to the FBI Friday morning, he said.
>
> Police said about $6,000 was taken in the robbery.
>
> Police and FBI officials were continuing to investigate Friday as Schock appeared in court.
>
> Schock appeared to have been moving from place to place, living with friends, and has no known address of his own, FBI spokesman Ross Rice said.
>
> As banks are federally insured institutions, all bank robberies fall within the jurisdiction of the FBI. The bureau investigates these robberies in conjunction with local law enforcement, Rice said.[11]

The *Chicago Tribune's* local for Arlington Heights, *The Pioneer Press* of the same date had more detail and portrayed David as a hapless bank robber:

> Arlington Heights police arrested a 23-year-old man for allegedly robbing a bank on Dec. 4 after police said they found him holding an exploded dye pack and the stolen money.
>
> David Schock, described as homeless, was charged Dec. 5 with bank robbery for allegedly taking $6,066 from Chase Bank, at 43 E. Gold Road, Arlington Heights, said FBI spokesman Ross Rice.

---

[11]Glad, Frieda. "Man arrested in Arlington Heights bank robbery," 5 December 2008, *Daily Herald,* https://www.dailyherald.com/news/20081206/man-arrested-in-arlington-heights-bank-robbery?cid=search

A man with very short black hair, wearing a black leather "Bulls" basketball jacket and blue jeans, approached a teller at about 2 p.m. Dec. 4. He handed a teller a note which said he had a gun and would shoot if the teller did not give him money, according to court documents.

The court documents stated the teller gave the man all the money in the drawer. The teller also gave the robber a dye pack. The man ran away.

When the police arrived a minute later, a customer who had just finished a transaction at the bank's drive-through window described seeing the suspect run south and jump a fence. The witness then reported seeing a large puff of red smoke.

The Arlington Heights police broadcast the description of the suspect, and an officer spotted a man wearing a black "Bulls" jacket about 500 yards from the bank.

When the officers identified themselves to the suspect, who was later identified as Schock, he ran away but was quickly caught, the court documents stated. The officers found $3,205 and an exploded dye pack in a white bag under Schock's jacket. The police also reported there was red dye on his pants.

The teller who was robbed identified Schock as the man who had taken the money, police said.

Arlington Heights police officers also found about $2,467 near the fence which the witness reported the fleeing suspect had climbed.

In federal court today, Schock pleaded not guilty to the charge of bank robbery. His next court date is Dec. 10.[12]

Twenty-three, just 23-years-old.

The court records laid out the case against him pretty well in the affidavit attached to the complaint:

Case: 1:08-cr-01006 Document #: 1 Filed: 12/05/08

I, Craig J. Heidenreich, being duly sworn, do hereby state and depose as follows:

1. I am a Special Agent with the Federal Bureau of Investigation ("FBI") and have been so employed for approximately three years. I am currently assigned to the violent crimes squad of the FBI's Rolling Meadows office. My duties include the investigation of bank robberies and other violent crimes.

---

[12] Fornek, Kimberly. 5 December 2008, *The Pioneer Press.*

2. I make this affidavit based upon my personal knowledge, my participation in this investigation, reports I have read, and conversations I have had with others who have personal knowledge of the events and circumstances described herein. The information below is provided for the limited purpose of establishing probable cause that, on or about December 4, 2008, DAVID SCHOCK did, by intimidation, take from the person and presence of bank employees, approximately $6,066.00 in United States Currency belonging to and in the care, custody, control, management, and possession of the Chase Bank, located at 43 East Golf Road, Arlington Heights, Illinois, the deposits of which were then insured by the Federal Deposit Insurance Corporation (FDIC), in violation of Title 18, United States Code, Section 2113 (a). Because the information set forth below is for the limited purpose of establishing probable cause in support of a criminal complaint, it does not contain all the facts of which I am aware related to this investigation.

3. On December 4, 2008, at approximately 2:00 p.m., the Chase Bank, located at 43 East V Golf Road, Arlington Heights, Illinois (the "Bank") was robbed.

4. Teller A, who was working at the Bank on December 4, 2008, observed a white male ("Subject") approach Teller A's teller counter at approximately 2:00 pm. According to Teller A, Subject was approximately 6'0", of slim build, approximately 25 years old, had very short black hair, was wearing blue jeans, a white shirt with blue stripes, and a black leather "Bulls" jacket with red stripes on the sleeves. According to Teller A, Subject approached the teller counter and handed Teller A a note which read something to the effect of "I have a gun in my coat, give me all the money you have or you will die." Teller A gave Subject all of the United States Currency from Teller A's teller drawer, which included a dye pack. Teller A saw Subject exit the bank after receiving the money.

5. At approximately the same time the robbery occurred, Witness A had just finished a transaction in the Bank drive-thru when Witness A noticed Subject running south from the Bank. Witness A saw Subject jump a fence, at which time Witness A saw a large puff of red smoke. Witness A exited the drive-thru and noticed an Arlington Heights police car driving into the Bank parking lot at a high rate of speed. Witness A approached the Arlington Heights police officer and advised what had happened. Witness A described Subject as a white male with black hair who was wearing a black jacket. The Arlington Heights Police Department relayed the description of Subject and the direction of travel to its responding vehicles.

6. Shortly after receiving the radio call, an Arlington Heights police officer noticed a man matching the physical description of Subject, wearing a black "Bulls" jacket, walking approximately 500 yards from the Bank. The Arlington Heights officers approached Subject and identified themselves. Subject started running away from the officers but was quickly apprehended.

While conducting a safely check on Subject, officers found $3,205.00 and an exploded dye pack in a white bag underneath Subject's black "Bulls" jacket. Officers also noticed what appeared to be red dye on the Subject's pants.

7. Arlington Heights police officers brought Teller A to the area where Subject was being detained for the purpose of conducting a show up identification. Teller A identified Subject as being the person who robbed the Bank. Subject was subsequently arrested by the Arlington Heights Police Department. Subject later identified himself as DAVID SCHOCK.

8. An employee of the Bank informed me that the Bank possesses a video surveillance system. Subject was captured by that system during the robbery. I have reviewed the video surveillance from the Bank, and it reveals that the robber was a white male who had short black hair and was wearing a black jacket with red stripes. The robber's face is visible in the surveillance photographs. I have compared still photographs taken from this surveillance video to DAVID SCHOCK and they appear to be the same person.

9. Arlington Heights police officers also recovered $2,566.90 near the site where Witness A saw Subject jump the fence.

10. According to a regional manager of the Bank, the man who robbed the Bank took $6,066.

11. According to the regional manager of Chase Bank, on December 4, 2008, at the time of the robbery, the Federal Deposit Insurance Corporation insured the accounts of the Chase Bank, located at 43 East Golf Road, Arlington Heights, Illinois.

Conclusion

12. Based on the facts set forth above, I respectfully submit that there is probable cause to believe that DAVID SCHOCK robbed the Chase Bank located at 43 East Golf Road, Arlington Heights, Illinois, on December 4, 2008, in violation of Title 18 United States Code Section 2113(a).

FURTHER AFFIANT SAYETH NOT.

Craig J. Heidenreich, Special Agent
Federal Bureau of Investigation

Subscribed to and sworn before me this 5th day of December, 2008,
United State Magistrate Judge Michael T. Mason

Bail was denied, but none would have been forthcoming in any event.

And what we didn't know then but would only learn much later, years later, was that David had been arrested before all this, November 7th, for stealing a satellite radio from a Dodge Caravan in Mount Prospect. He sat in jail for nearly a month, until December 3rd, THE DAY BEFORE his arrest for bank robbery. On Dec. 3—the day before the robbery—he pled guilty, was given 18 months' probation, and ordered to pay $500 in restitution and a $560 fine.

As well, there was a petition for violation of probation for an earlier arrest in March. He had been charged with resisting arrest. So, Dec. 3 a warrant was issued.

Why didn't he go back to jail then and there? And what of an assessment made during the November incarceration that he had an ongoing problem with alcohol and other drugs? The legal system's own assessors indicated that he was not in a fit state to be out on the streets on his own.

At the time, we knew nothing of the November arrest. I'd learn more about it later.[13]

Kathy wrote to Daniel to let him know that David had been arrested for the bank robbery. She ended her letter with, "Well, at least we know where both our boys are this Christmas." That wasn't cold; it was true. Had David actually had a weapon and brandished it, he could well have been dead on the ground. That he wasn't, and was in fact treated with care and regard, says much. I always will be grateful to Special Agent Heidenreich for allowing and encouraging that phone call from my son.

The formal charges against him were filed Dec. 18, 2008.

David was first housed at the Metropolitan Correctional Center, 71 W. Van Buren St. Chicago IL, 60605. His registration number was 40885-424.

Later he was moved to the Kankakee County Jail as Prisoner # 411 484, 3050 Justice Way, Kankakee, IL, while awaiting his court date.

Kathy had let both David and Daniel know that if they wanted the regular small stipends to hit their commissary accounts that they needed to write at least once a month. And I promised them that for every letter they sent I would return one. It worked. David wrote to us. I have preserved here his idiosyncratic spelling and grammar. They reveal to me some of his intelligence. While he had both been denied writing skills as a young child and later denied himself by his truncated education, there was no lack of intelligence. I have transcribed all his letters from prison; these letters are the last tangible reminder and remainder of what he was thinking.

---

[13] And this will come up again in more detail subsequently.

Dear Mom and Dad

I miss both of you and love guys so much. I'm in the progress of accepting what I've done. I have strayed so far I don't even know who I'm any more. I feel like I let everybody win who said or thought because the way I grew up this is where I'd end up, like I am some kind of statistic. I only blame my self. I let my past get the best of me. Its to late now to think about that I could have done different.

I can't change the past. I have been doing a lot of thinking about my future, and what I want out of life. Its not this. I see my dad in me and my brother and it scares me. I need to break the cycle.

I'm in Kankakee which is alright except I don't know where I am. Someone told me its south of the city. The federal system is way different than the state. There are manditory time limit between court dates like in the state. Even once you get sentenced there no time limit on when they have to move you. theres people been here for 11 months. One guy has been sentenced for 6 months and is still here. I think all the federal prisons are full. Most of the people are here for drugs, but not no little stuff, the big time dealer and gang leaders. I looking forward to going to prision Its way better than where I'm at. They have school, and other programs. At fed prisions you last year you can go to a halfway house, if your good. People have told me that its alot better than state prison. Better food, cleaner. You can't smoke which is good.

I just got moved to a dorm. It houses about fifty people Before that I was in a cell with 1 other person. I was locked down all day except for a hour in the morning and a hour at night.

Anywaz thanks for the support I can use all I can get. Send me some pics of you guys and the ones of me and Maggie.

I love you lots

Your son
David Schock

PS tell Maggie to send pics.

Merry Christmas

Kankakee is about 60 miles south of Chicago, as Kathy wrote back to him:

> . . . [O]n Interstate 57 according to the city's website. It has four fire stations, 50 firemen, 74 police officers, and 118 miles of sewers (bet you really wanted to know that!). I remember driving through there one time and it seems like it was good-sized town way out in the country if I remember correctly. When you were

describing the people you are locked up with, I was wondering how Christmas was for the teller at the bank. That had to be so scary to get that note and wonder if you were going to be alive to go home to your family that night. I hope she is OK.

David had no idea that—even without a weapon, just passing over a note demanding money—that he'd be on the hook for murder if the teller had suffered a heart attack and died. He responded with more reflection on his life. Midway through he addressed the matter of the teller:

Jan 13, 2009

Dear Mom and Dad

How you guys doing. I miss you guys so much, and wish I could see you, but I think I'm where I'm supposed to be. This is Gods way of telling me to slow down, and move on with my life. This a time for me to reflect on how I have lived my life so far, from my childhood to now. In this short time I've been here I relize that me and my brother are liveing the same way we did when we were kids Just in reverse. Were going tru the same miserable life but in my dads shoes. I've learned when living this life, it' progresively gets worse and worse. I do belevie unless me and my brother make drastic changes in our life style, that death is the end result like my dad, aunt and uncle. I do belevie me and daniel carry the bourden of stopping this visous cycle. JungYi said it first and I feel the same way. I'm scared to have kids. I beleive that we can do it. were the type of kids that can't take your word for it, we have to do it the hard way and see it our selfs. Anyways sorry for being so serious, I have been doing a lot of thinking and soul searching. I could fill up a thousand pages with all the things that have been going tru my mind. One thing is for sure I rather be in here than be free and live how I was living on the outside, and it sucks here. I'm going to do everything I can to better myself while I'm here: mind, body and soul. I'm working out and running to get in the best physical shape of my life. I'm reading and gonna go back to school. I'm going to bible study and and AA meetings. What ever resources they give me I gonna use. I know and accepted that I'm gonna be locked up for a while, but I didn't get this way or end up in prison over night. So its going to be a full time job fixing my self, but like I said I have nothing but time. The day I get out of Prison is going to be like my rebirth. I'm gonna start all over, and leave my past behind me. Its only gonna be a memory of what I don't want to be any more. Its a long time away before I have to worry about getting out, but I want to make sure I'm ready and I did every thing I could to better myself.

A lot of people come in sleep and play cards all day and leave the same way they came in. Those are the same people doing thier third or fourth bids.

I wish there was a way for me to apologize to that teller at the bank. I would have never done a thing to her, but she didn't know that. I think its best though if I leave that alone.

I been talking to some of the people that have already been to the fed Joint. They say you can go to college or get a trade. Depending on how much time I get I might want to get a degree instead of just a trade. Im looking at 3-5 years with 2 months off good time for every year. Plus you get 3 months halfway house for every year, for up to a year. So if I get 3 years I can get 6 months off for good time and nine months in a halfway house. Its all up to the Judge and God how much time I aculy get. I'm going to be in Kankakee for a while, at least 8 months maybe more. I don't even have a court date. The feds take their time.

Please send me pics. I want pics of every body you guys. JungYi and Daniel. When your locked up pictures mean a lot. When I get to prison you can pay to have you pic taken, so I send you guys a pic of me.

Send me Daniels info I can write him I just got to fill out a special request slip.

I can't wait to hear from your guys.

Love David

With David thinking of his future and knowing that it would be some time until he was settled in a federal prison, I wrote to him Jan. 28, 2009, about Daniel's choices to seek training behind bars. These were things David also might think of.

> I have written to Daniel urging him to stay in prison as long as it takes for him to earn a welding certificate . . . even if they want to parole him! He's been learning rapidly . . . as he often does; he is—as you are—an intelligent young man who is capable of a whole lot. And learning a trade will help him. This kind of training is worth almost anything. He COULD come out of there with a skill that will let him make money for the rest of his life. And if it takes one or two more months, he might ask them to allow him to stay; mastering a skilled trade would certainly help him to avoid returning to prison. Now, I'm pretty sure what I'm saying is not what you'll hear often recommended. He and you, David, need to learn something that will offer you a future.
>
> Initially, Daniel thought about taking up something in business. When I saw him I asked him if he thought that people would be eager to hire him in an office where there likely would be financial transactions. He guessed not. So I urged him to take up a skill and he managed to get into welding. I'd urge you to do the same if you have the opportunity.
>
> I thought your comments about you needing to be in prison were especially insightful. I grieve because you have committed such a serious crime. I am relieved that no one was hurt . . . you included. While I can wish that you'd avoided the crime I agree that you are better off there than drinking and homeless on the streets. That's such a hard way to live. Sobriety also is hard, but it's a choice you're going to have to make if you want to live. It will be some time

before you're out, and just now there's a hostile economic climate out here. Unemployment in Michigan is now more than ten percent. That means that for every ten people who walk past me on the street probably one of them will be looking for a job. Wages are falling . . . but so are housing prices. I think we truly are in a financial depression, not just a recession. But it really doesn't matter what you call it . . . in fact, one comic said "It's a recession when your neighbor loses his job; it's a depression when you lose yours."

Jack and Gracie send their best wags and a bark.

Mom, as you know, is assiduous in sending some money each month. She's the best. She's a more regular correspondent than I, but we both read your letters and we talk about you every day. You are in my prayers, right along with Daniel and JungYi. We love each one of you.

Love,

David B. Schock

Our prayer lives are private, but both of us kept the kids close to our hearts and we talked with God about them every day. Never once did either one of us say anything other than our choice for adoption was the right choice. No matter what, these were our children.

David wrote again, updating us on his legal status and his interior reflections.

Dear Dad

How have you been. Its the same old thing here. Still waiting to see what their going to offer me. Have you been busy. You said you were working on a project about an unsolved murder what going on with that. [. . .]

I've been playing a lot of basket ball, and I'm getting pretty good. My wind is coming back, since I haven't been smoking. A couple years away might do me some good. Sometimes I just get so angry. When I start thinking about everything, bout growing up until now, I started hating everybody and I don't want to talk to any one. I have a friend who reads the bible with me. Its been keeping sane in here. I've done a lot of bad things. Anyways I want to do better and I'll do all I can. I'm gonna keep reading the bible. Pray for me and keep you my prayers.

Love

David Schock

And another letter:

> Dear Mom and Dad
>
> How are you guys doing. I doing alright I have another court date on the 15th. I'm not sure what it is for, but I'll tell what happens. I can't wait to get all the court stuff over with so I can start my time. At the fed prison they have a music room. It has all kinds of different instruments. There a couple of people here that have done time in federal prison. One of the differences between federal and state is in state you can sit around and sleep all day, in federal you have to work 8 hours a day or go to school full time. the only thing better about state is you only have to serve 50 % of your time if it is a non violent crime. I've been reading law books everyday. I know more than my layer about my case. Every time I ask him a question he doesn't know. He trys to put in for downward departures that I have to tell him I don't qualify for. Everything that we ask for so far I told my layer to ask for. I told him to ask for a phsyc evaluation, cause the fact that I take phsyc meds and at the time I was off my meds, it could help my case. My lawyer wanted to say that I was intoxicated when I commited the crime, I had to tell him that there are not deduction of points or downward departures for being an addit or being under the influence at the time of the crime. There is a drug program that you can take to get some time off, which I don't qualify for which my lawyer was trying to get for me. Since at the time I was homeless, that could help me out, because I did it under extreme circumstances and I was under financial duress. I found all these things by reading law books on my case. The first advise I got from all the other inmates when I told them I a had a public defender was start reading the law books and research my own case. He told me everytime he was going to visit me before court. he has not visited me once. Its OK as long as the Judge doesn't give me an outrougeous amount of time. I got a pretty good idea of what I looking at.[14]
>
> I find law very interesting. I find it irronic how two people getting charged with the same case, one can get probation and the other gets three years. I've seen people in here for conspiracy which carries 10 to 30, someone got 15 years another 10 and the other 7 and they were all on the same conspiracy charge.
>
> How are your dogs, Jacks getting old. Hows lenny doing. Hey Dad what kind of projects are you working on. Are you still doing movies on unsolved murders. Dad I can't wait till I get to prison, so I can get to the music room. My goal is write an whole album. I figure I will probley never again have so much time to to devote to stuff like music and school. When I get out supporting my self will come first, then what ever time is extra I can use for school and music. I courious to see how much I can acomplish with alcohol out of the way.

---

[14] At the time we didn't have any knowledge by which to judge David's court-appointed attorney, Pablo deCastro. Later I would assess his performance as far more than adequate. Even David would rethink his earlier impressions.

Mom are you still working at the church. Thanks for telling me about you and your sister going back to school, it makes me reliize that it is never to late. I told JungYi this, I been on my own since I was 15 but I'm still like a kid always trying to stay with someone instead of being a man and getting my own place. When I get out I'm not asking for help from any body. I'm gonna do it my self. When you can support your self you don't have to worry about where your gonna stay, or how your gonna feed yourself. Anyways just stuff I have been thinking about. I can't wait to hear from you.

Love

David Schock

Stewed in drugs and alcohol, a survivor of a lot of early and recent trauma, David was unlikely to have realized that until he turned 18, we had made as sure as possible that he had shelter and food. Never had he been abandoned. Never. But there was little doubt it felt like it in his mind. Kathy and I both believe you never let a lie stand, so when he made the claim, she wrote back:

February 1, 2009

Hi David—

It was interesting to read your nice, long letter. I can understand why you would have a special interest in studying the law right now. You have a personal interest in your case! While you are feeling anxious to get Court out of the way, all of your days in jail should count towards your sentence in the end. Daniel was not happy when we refused to bail him out or hire a private attorney for him because he thought he would get a shorter sentence if he had a different attorney. That's what people told him in the jail. I told him that there is a range for the crime(s) you are charged with that can vary with the specifics of the crime. For example, what your note said may make a difference in sentencing. The sentencing guidelines are pretty straightforward and specific. Daniel received the standard range for his crime. Since he was homeless and without a job or money, it didn't make any sense to bail him out since he had nowhere to go and we didn't think he would show up for Court if he did (this is what it means when you post bail—that you promise the person will show up for Court). As we pointed out to him, his "waiting" time for Court counted toward his sentence; he says he's glad now that it worked out that way. You might be interested to know that people get different sentences for "conspiracy" depending on the underlying crime they participated with others in, the specific details of their own actions, as well as their own criminal history. For example, if you are doing a robbery with a group of people and someone gets killed, everyone can be charged with murder even if they did not shoot the gun. If you are ever under "financial duress" in the future, I strongly recommend a homeless shelter and a food bank. The Court isn't likely to buy "financial duress" as a reason for leniency when you rob a bank. In law school, they teach you that <u>all the facts of the crime</u> lead to the decision.

      I was curious to know what type of "psych meds" you are taking right now? What are they for? How long were you off them before you were locked up? You hadn't mentioned anything about this to me before. Have you already been to Court since you went in Kankakee? You mentioned that the lawyer did not meet with you before you went.

      When you say that you were "on my own since I was 15," I think you have rewritten your personal history of your teenage years if you are saying you were taking care of yourself on your own without our help. This simply isn't true and is not consistent with the facts. You were here living at our house and attending Grand Haven High School until February 26, 2001 (age 16 then). On that date, and with your agreement, I sent you to stay with my brother John in Windsor as an alternative to placing you in boarding school. I paid John for your room, board, supervision, and cigarettes, so you were not "on your own" there either. You lived with John and attended Walkerville High School in Windsor from March 2001 until November 1, 2001 when you left school after a confrontation with the teacher about lighting a lighter in class. You continued to live at John's until January 26, 2002 (age 17 then) when there was a confrontation with swearing and threatening John's children, and he asked you to leave. John took you to City Detox on January 28, 2002, at your request and you stayed there for ten days, and then refused to go to a 90 or 21-day treatment center for substance abuse. You stayed with Grandma Neville for a few days. Since you wouldn't go back to school or get treatment or go to boarding school, I asked you what you wanted to do and you said "go to Florida." The problem on our end was that the police would not do anything because you were already 17. So we put you on a bus to Fort Lauderdale on February 9, 2002 (age 17). You said you would get a job there (I don't think you ever looked for a job). I sent money Western Union ($100) when you arrived. You stayed with someone you met on the bus for a couple weeks and then went to Covenant House on February 23, 2002, at my suggestion. You bounced in and out of Covenant House until May 18, 2002, and I sent Covenant House money each week you stayed there to pay for your room and board. You were arrested for shoplifting during this time. On May 18, 2002, you called me and said you were tired of being on the streets of Fort Lauderdale and wanted to go to boarding school. I bought you a bus ticket to Mobile, Alabama, and Tommy from Bethel came and picked you up on May 19th from the bus station in Mobile. You stayed at Bethel from then until the month after you turned 18 (and we paid them a lot of money for your room and board and supervision). At that point, I told them you were on your own because you were legally an adult. You went to work and got your own place and stayed in Mississippi until sometime in July 2003 when your bio mom came and picked you up and took you to Jung Yi's house. I kept detailed notes about everything that happened during this whole period (and I was in very frequent contact with Covenant House, the Courts, and Police in Florida), so you can ask me if you would like to know other details about this period.

My brother, Jeff, died this morning.

Love, Mom

So, David had been there when Kathy's sister was dying; he'd left just weeks before her passing. That was in 2000. And by this time in 2009 Kathy had lost not only her sister and younger brother, but her older brother and her mother. And there were other losses, too. David wrote back acknowledging his mother's loss.

Dear Mom

I'm so sorry to hear about your brother Jeff. I know you and Neville family must be in alot of pain. I will keep all of you in my prayers. I know Letting go of a loved is one of the hardest things a person goes through, I tell my self now their in a better place where theres no suffering?

Do you think the economy will get better in a couple of years? I hope by the time I get out of prison the economy will be much better. I'm already gonna have enough trouble getting a job with or without a good economy. I gonna do everything I can to better my chances of getting a good job, while I'm locked up.

You were wondering what kind of meds I take. Zoloft, Kolotapin, and Serequel, I'm not sure if I spelled Kolotipin right. When I was working my insurance paid for them, but when lost my insurance I could not afford them them any more. I get them for free here. They been helping me out a lot, being in this situation and all. When I go to prison I gonna try get off my meds, because I don't wan't to become dependent on them.

Maybe I'm a little off about my past. But I know John kick me out after the 9th grade. I was in folorida for while before I want to bethel. When I got arrested for shopping lifting I was in Juviy and they were gonna send me back to mighigan. They put me in a boys home and I ran away. If I was seveenteen they would have tried me as a adult. I might be off, that just how I rember it. Anyways that stuff is in the Past and doesn't matter to me any more.

Love

David Schock

We had known that he had sought some kind of community mental health help after he lost his job and while he was still outside, but was this the result? Zoloft (sertraline HCI), Klonopin (clonazepam), and Seroquel (quetiapine fumarate), a real mix for depression, anxiety, and bipolar disorder. Which of his symptoms were caused by his alcoholism, attendant mental illness, trauma? The list of meds was disheartening.

Dear Mom and Dad.

How are you guys doing. I hope your doing well. I hope mom is feeling better. I doing fine, same old thing every day. Still in the process of being sentenced. They offered me a plea agreement for pleing guilty, of 46 months. It still going to be a while before I'm sentenced. The Chicago Federal system is back up. The real Federal Jail is in down town Chicago and its a sky scraper and its pacted so they use 5 different counties that I know of to house chicago feds. One of my friends just left to prison, hes been here to 2 and a half years. Its good that all this time counts but your in one room with out windows, in prison I found out that you have to work 8 hours of the day unless your in school. You get to go outside everyday. Its a better but its still 'prision.'

Everyday before I go to sleep I think about my past and about my future. I realize where I went wrong I lost passion for life. Not just with everyday things, but with things that are supposed to be fun, like going to beach, movie the mall. I was misserable on the inside but pretend everything was fine. Drinking to feel normal.

When I look back I was the happiest when I was living simple. like when I lived in mississippi. I did not have a lot, different have alchol problems and then littlest things made me happy. I want to move to new place and start fresh. Feds are eligible for up to year of half way house. I going to ask to get moved some place besides Chicago. My cell mate told me that they let him move because he said he wanted to get away from his old friends and have a fresh start. Anywaz thing I been thinking about.

I miss you guys so so much and cant' wait to hear rom you.

Send me more pics.

Love

David
Schock

. . . His time in Mississippi, with Joe Havard of the fence company and the little house in the cattle grazing lands. It may have been the best time in his life, away from drugs and alcohol.

Every time he was to show up to court, he was moved from his cell in Kankakee back to the Chicago holding pen of the Metropolitan Correctional Center.

Dear Mom and Dad

How are your guys doing. I'm back in Chicago, and doing the best I can considering the situation. I have court on the 26. I'll tell you what happens.

Everything is very slow motion here. I talked to Maggie for the firs time in about 6 months. She started crying and telling me how much she loves and misses me, and asking me why I did this to her. I didn't have an answer. The thing that that hurts the most, worst than prison is hearing Maggie cry, or having to call you guys to tell you I just robed a bank. I think about it all the time. I know times are rough for you guys to. I been praying for you guys. Things will get better I have faith. I think tough times and the struggles we go through give people more chacter. I hope work picks up. You guys do your best and I'll do mine.

Love

David Schock

P.S. you send me a book on how to write poetry and songs.

At that moment he realized that his actions had deeply affected others. That realization might not last, but for the moment, I conjectured, it was helping him in the right direction.

Dear Mom and Dad

Hows everything going. I can't see but I watch the news and it warming up outside. It must be nice outside, I'd love just to go for a walk, and see the a sunrise. Its crazy how you miss the simple things in life. Sometimes I just day dream about the out side. The good and the bad. All I ca'nt do is just think about what I'm going to do when I get out Theres people here who say thy will give me a job when I get out, but I'm not going to relie on that. There are a lot of white collar criminals in here who have the own bussiness but I'm not sure if that the kind of people I want to work for.

I've learned the magic of reading. When I'm reading something that intreest me, I can escape from this place. I've read all the good books from here, the only way to get a book is to order from Amazon or something. Every body here gets these stupid hood books sent here about drug dealing and living in the hood. Their like rap cds on books. If you could send me a book that would be awsome.

I watch MMA, its my favorite sport. It stands for Mix martial arts. I like to read more about it. Also Brazilian JuJitsu If you can thats be great.

How are your guys doing. Could you send me some more pictures. thanks for telling me that Maggie called, I so glad to hear you guys talk. She a good girl and I'm happy shes doing good. Id rather her be happy without me than miserable with me. She has problems too trying to fit in and life in general maybe you can help her like have made me relize things. She a special girl you'll find the more you talk with her, I hope you guys become friends.

Do know about probation and where your aloud to move. I don't know if this would be bad for but, I wanted to move to LA, or Phoniz. for some reason I like the desert and being on the coast, but I don't want to go back to floridia. Anyways things I been thinking about.

Love
your
son
David Schock

So, you couldn't just wrap up some books and send them along. It makes sense . . . you could smuggle almost anything inside a book you'd fiddled with. There are tales of inmates' friends soaking pages corners in blotter acid, something to give a little thrill and to help pass an inmate's otherwise interminable day. And there was always the possibility of metal objects secreted in book spines. So, it would be Amazon or nothing. I ordered up and had sent a complete collection of *The Chronicles of Narnia*. Here was David's response:

Dear Mom and Dad

How are you guys doing thank you, I got the book you sent me. Its one big book with all the seven stories in it with a lion on the front. I almost half way done with it. I feel like I can get away from this world when I really get into a book. Its the same with music. I cant wait to play a instrument I don't even care what it is, as long as it make noise.

Im dont know what to do. Maggie calls you and calls my best friend to see what going with me. He to told me she wrote write me because I'll call my friends but I won't call her. Even if I did call her I would't know what to say. Maybe its better f I stop thinking about it, but you know, it hard.

It gonna be weird when I get back out there on the dating. If I start hiting it off with some one whens good time to tell them your a bank Robber. But then again some girls like that. HaHa

I been working out, I gained a lot of weight. [. . .] all muscle. The food here is so much better than Cook County. You get a balonga samwich everyday for lunch and slop, real slop everyday in Cook County. Theirs 16,000 inmate in Cook. It sucks there.

Hey i wrote JungYi a letter but I think I might have messed up her address. Could you please give it t me.

I have 3 goals in prsion, these arent the life changeing type, write a Book, a album, and get in the best shape ever in my life.

I love you two very much. In closing this a question for both of you. When you guys decided to adopt us. Did you think it be the normal high school then collaeg routine, or in the back of you mind did you know it be this way for me and Daniel. You can't be surpprised the odds were overwhelming against us. Anywaz I do love you both so much.

Your son

David Schock

And there was the question: "Did you know it would be like this?"

April 22, 2009

Dear David:

I've told Mom that I will be thinking about books that might delight . . . books not just for young people, but for adults. For instance, I reread the Narnian Chronicles about once every two years. There are lessons there I need to have refreshed that deal with the wonder of living. Lewis also wrote a really amazing science fiction trilogy (three books): *Out of the Silent Planet*, *Perelandra*, and *The Hideous Strength*. You might very much like them.

I also was thinking about your growth and maturation. Did you know that when young people start doing drugs and alcohol that they stop maturing at the age they start drugging? For a 14 year old, who doesn't sober up until he's 25, that means that he has to start at the emotional age of 14 to grow again. That's not what he knows or how smart he is . . . but how he emotionally responds to what's going on around him. These people often have to go back and be both children and to parent themselves at the same time. Difficult at best, but it can be done. One of the biggest lessons is to understand that persistence is everything. There will be days when it feels that all is lost, that there can be no hope. But the parenting adult has to step in and say: "Let's just keep on until tomorrow and we'll see; it might be a little better." The adult also has to tell the child to go a little easier on himself . . . that his failings do not make him a failure, that everybody does stupid things, especially when he is young, that there is hope for improvement in circumstance and understanding.

You have asked a question I have long been anticipating and I have thought over the years how I might respond. I'll give it my best shot. Tomorrow I might add something more, so this is FOR TODAY but tomorrow would be very similar.

Yes, we knew that you were badly scarred by what had happened in your lives. We knew there would be many challenges and would likely face some big problems. We knew the deck was stacked against you and against us in adopting you. But we had been asked. Mom HEARD God ask her if we'd do this for Him. She was driving at the time and this voice came out of the radio "You have to get a home study done NOW." All the rest followed, including my vision of a sibling trio . . . an older sister and two boys. The adoption guy thought we were a little screwy until you showed up. Then he got it.

So, knowing all that we knew, trusting there was plenty more that we didn't but might not think was a lot of fun, we went ahead. Really, we had two choices: yes or no. God would not have punished us for choosing "No," but what has happened would not have happened if we had.

Imagine our thoughts when you all had been here less than two weeks and JungYi was arrested for shoplifting?

Or what it might have signified when our middle child would night after night have to seek out his younger brother in order to fall asleep in the same room. The reason: He was terrified of aliens . . . powerful beings that would take him away. Well, what EXACTLY had happened to him? Hadn't he been abducted by aliens? And not once, but several times?

. . . And our youngest son who defied any thing or any one to make an impact on him. He was resolute that he would not be affected. So he would lie, steal, cheat to get what he wanted because otherwise it would not be his. Other people could NOT be trusted; they will abandon you.

We saw all this early on. In one humorous moment I said to Mom that while I realized that having you three was going to be a lot of work I didn't realize it was going to be so unrelenting. We were outnumbered. The only down time was when you were asleep. Even meals were a gamble: not one of you could sit calmly at the table for an entire dinner. You always had to be jumping up to do something.

But there were other times, too, that were fun and funny. We spent a lot of time at the YMCA. We went places and did things. There was a lot of music, there were educated people who really had something to say to you (like Bill Mulligan[15]).

And there was no question that we loved you. We didn't hesitate for a minute to finalize the adoption. In fact we wanted to make sure that was done before you experienced your first real Michigan winter; we didn't want YOU to back out.

Through it all, we learned we had to become ISP—Industrial Strength Parents. Stuff like: "If you think it's a good idea to do drugs, we'll agree enough that we think everybody should know it. Grandma would be interested." Or talking bluntly with your teachers about what was happening. Or with the parents of your friends. We didn't hide anything from you or from them.

---

[15] William H. Mulligan, Jr., Ph.D., is a historian and remains a good and trusted friend. He was great with the kids and they loved learning anything from him.

Our primary purpose was to be of benefit to you. But along the way there was a surprise we hadn't counted on: Mom and I benefited, too. We grew in ways that NEVER would have happened otherwise. Those are great gifts. We would do it again. Maybe we'd do it even better if we knew then what we know now. Maybe not, though. We did the best we could.

And how do we look at it all now? Certainly, with some sorrow for your addictions and actions that led to imprisonment. But that's where you need to be for now. I would any day have you in prison than dead . . . and that always is the other possibility.

I believe with all my heart that your life can be turned around, that it can leave you as a happy and contented person, someone glad to be alive and who understands that everything that has happened to him can be put to work in his life as a constructive force. I believe that you have a wonderful future.

Our role in your life is both the same and different. We love you and believe that you can become whatever kind of person you want to be. But we are no longer the parents of little children. We will not play Mommy and Daddy to you and Daniel. We are not where you will live when either of you gets out. But we are adults who will treat you as adults and who rejoice every time you make an adult and mature decision. We pray for you, we root for you, we cheer you on. Simply, we love you and want the best for you.

And we would not make any other choice than to volunteer to be your parents . . . still.

Love,

David B. Schock

It was true. We believed in the power of healing and love. We still do.

Dear Dad

HAPPY FATHER'S DAY

How are you doing. wanted to say happy father's day. You probley not to proud of me right now. but I <u>promise</u> someday you will be. I hope your fathers day is great. I'm proud to have you as a dad and I luv u and mom very much. You raised 3 semi-good kids. We will get better. At least you got one thats doing good, better than nothing LOL.

I hope your bussiness picks up. I wonder if playing a lot of gigs. I can't wait till I get to play an instrument. I don't even care what it is. Music is such a great gift from God. Speaking of God I've been going to church and bible study every night.

It helps me with my anxiety, and to be at peace. Every body here prays to go home, I pray to be the strength to make it through this cause I know I'm not going home; at least not right now.

I hope Jack and Mrs. Wiggles[16] are doing alright. I love you Dad and I love you Mom.

David Schock

At that point, David was planning to enter a plea, and he knew that if it was accepted, he likely would be sentenced to serve the 46 months he had earlier calculated.

Dear Mom and Dad

How are things going right now. I've been moved to Kankakee. I got my Narnia book back. I'm reading it again. I like it better here. I'm in a dorm. In Chicago its two man cells. When I get locked in a cell, my nerves start going and I can't sit still. I pace some times. these are some things I'll never forget. On the 8th of this month I go to sighn my plea. My lawyer is a lyier, I wish I had a paid laywer. Its two days before I have to sighn a plea I have never seen yet, or decided to take my case to trial. He always promises to come see me and never does. He shows up 5 minutes before court. Anywaz I try not to stress about it to much. Have any advice mom on what I can do. When you write my Kankakee number is 411484. Not alot going on here when I sighn my plea, I tell you how much time I sighned for.

Dear Mom and Dad

I have some news on my case. I went to court on the 8th, and I sighned my plea. The Plea I sighned was for 46-57. Thats where I fall in the Sentencing Guideline range. But some time back they passed law where the Judge doesn't have to follow the Guide lines. But my lawyer told me 9 times out of 10 that they do. My case carries 20 years. My lawyer has a couple things that he can argue on my behalf, that might get me a little time off. I'm getting nervous, because the moment of truth is coming up. On September 15, I go to get sentenced. I'm scared to go but happy at the same time, because it will be all over. I'm in a state of mind where I know they could give me the high end, and I'll just be a man have to except it. After all that I'll be going to one of those prisons scattered all over the US. I really don't care where they send me. I don't plan on having any visitors. As long as they have weights. Thats what goinging on with me right now. How are yall doing. Anything new. I hope both of your bussiness have been picking up. I watch the news and

---

[16] Mrs. Wiggles was the stray we adopted, Gracie....Gracie Maybelle Wigglebutt. The "Wigglebutt" was in honor of a very short tail that helped set her backfield in joyful motion.

people talk about how hard it is because they had to cut down on some of their luxerys, and how the economy is effecting them. I'd be happy living in a box and working at McDonalds, if I good be free. Jail has humbled me, I hope I feel the same way when I get out. Latly I've been staying to self and trying to reavaluate my life from the beginning. And I relize I'm right where I'm suppose to be. The odds were heavily stacked against me and brother. From all the stuff I been trough the social workers could have said He'll end up in prison someday. I Just did not relize till now, me and my brother are Just another statistic. I refuse be that and Im gonna do everything to to change that. As you can tell I've had a lot of my mind. I can't wait to hear from you, your son.

David Schock

The plea agreement laid out his crime but spelled out previous offenses of which we were unaware. We were not surprised, though; alcoholism results in a lot of crazy behavior. The agreement explained how widely the punishment could vary and how each other infraction added points to incarceration. The fact that he accepted responsibility took points away. We were able to get a copy of this record through a request to the federal court.

UNITED STATES DISTRICT COURT
NORTHERN DISTRICT OF ILLINOIS
EASTERN DIVISION

UNITED STATES OF AMERICA)   No. 08 CR 1006
vs.)
DAVID SCHOCK)   Judge Charles R. Norgle, Sr.

Plea Agreement

1. This Plea Agreement between the United States Attorney for the Northern District of Illinois, PATRICK J. FITZGERALD, and defendant DAVID SCHOCK, and his attorney, PABLO DeCASTRO, is made pursuant to Rule 11 of the Federal Rules of Criminal Procedure. The parties to this Agreement have agreed upon the following:

Charge in this case

2. The indictment in this case charges defendant SCHOCK with, by intimidation, taking from the person and presence of a bank employee approximately $6,066.00 in United States currency belonging to, and in the care, custody, control, management, and possession of a bank, namely, the Chase Bank, 43 E. Golf Road, Arlington Heights, Illinois, in violation of Title 18, United States Code, Section 2113(a).

3. Defendant has read the charge against him contained in the indictment, and that charge has been fully explained to him by his attorney.

4. Defendant fully understands the nature and elements of the crime with which he has been charged.

Charge to Which Defendant is Pleading Guilty

5. By this Plea Agreement, defendant agrees to enter a voluntary plea of guilty to the indictment. Then indictment charges defendant with bank robbery, in violation of Title 18, United States Code, Section 2113(a).

Factual Basis

6. Defendant SCHOCK will plead guilty because he is in fact guilty of the charge contained in the indictment. In pleading guilty, defendant admits the following facts and that those facts establish his guilt beyond a reasonable doubt:

On or about December 4, 2008, at Chicago, in the Northern District of Illinois, Eastern Division, defendant DAVID SCHOCK did, by intimidation, take from the person and presence of a bank employee approximately $6,066.00 in United States currency belonging to, and in the care, custody, control, management, and possession of a bank, namely, the Chase Bank, 43 E. Golf Road, Arlington Heights, Illinois, the deposits of which were then insured by the Federal Deposit Insurance Corporation, in violation of Title 18, United States Code, Section 2113(a).

Specifically, on December 4, 2008, at approximately 2 p.m., defendant SCHOCK entered Chase Bank, 43 E. Golf Road, Arlington Heights, Illinois and proceeded to the teller counter. Defendant then handed the teller a note, written on a deposit slip from the bank, which stated, among other things: "Be quiet or I will kill u [. . .] give me everything be cool or some [sic] will die." After receiving the note from defendant, the teller gave defendant approximately $6,066.00. Defendant then fled the bank, carrying the money. At the time of the bank robbery on December 4, 2008, the Chase Bank was insured by the Federal Deposit Insurance Corporation.

Maximum Statutory Penalties

7. Defendant understands that the charge to which he is pleading guilty carries the following statutory penalties:

> a. A maximum sentence of 20 years' imprisonment. This offense also carries a maximum fine of $250,000. Defendant further understands that the judge also may impose a term of supervised release of not more than three years.

b. In accord with Title 18, United States Code, Section 3013, defendant will be assessed $100 on the charge to which he has pled guilty, in addition to any other penalty imposed.

Sentencing Guidelines Calculations

8. Defendant understands that in imposing sentence the Court will be guided by the United States Sentencing Guidelines. Defendant understands that the Sentencing Guidelines are advisory, not mandatory, but that the Court must consider the Guidelines in determining a reasonable sentence.

9. For purposes of calculating the Sentencing Guidelines, the parties agree on the following points:

> a. **Applicable Guidelines**. The Sentencing Guidelines to be considered in this case are those in effect at the time of sentencing. The following statements regarding the calculation of the Sentencing Guidelines are based on the Guidelines Manual currently in effect, namely the November 2008 Guidelines Manual.
>
> b. **Offense Level Calculations**.
> i. The base offense level for the charge in the indictment is 20, pursuant to Guideline § 2B3.1(a).
>
> ii. The base offense level is increased by 2 levels because the property of a financial institution was taken, pursuant to Guideline § 2B3.1(b)(1).
>
> iii. The base offense level is increased by 2 levels because the defendant made a threat of death, pursuant to Guideline § 2B3.1(b)(2)(F).
>
> iv. Defendant has clearly demonstrated a recognition and affirmative acceptance of personal responsibility for his criminal conduct. If the government does not receive additional evidence in conflict with this provision, and if defendant continues to accept responsibility for his actions within the meaning of Guideline § 3E1.1(a), including
> by furnishing the United States Attorney's Office and the Probation Office with all requested financial information relevant to his ability to satisfy any fine that may be imposed in this case, a two-level reduction in the offense level is appropriate.
>
> v. In accord with Guideline § 3E1.1(b), defendant has timely notified the government of his intention to enter a plea of guilty, thereby permitting the government to avoid preparing for trial and

permitting the Court to allocate its resources efficiently. Therefore, as provided by Guideline § 3E1.l(b), if the Court determines the offense level to be 16 or greater prior to determining that defendant is entitled to a two-level reduction for acceptance of responsibility, the government will move for an additional one-level reduction in the offense level.

c. **Criminal History Category.** With regard to determining defendant's criminal history points and criminal history category, based on the facts now known to the government and stipulated below, defendant's criminal history points equal 5 and defendant's criminal history category is III:

i. On or about June 2, 2004, defendant was convicted of violating the liquor control act in Cook County, and sentenced to ten days imprisonment. This conviction does not result in the application of any criminal history points, pursuant to Guideline § 4A1.2(c)(2).

ii. On or about July 5, 2006, defendant was convicted of misdemeanor damage to property in Des Plaines, Illinois, and sentenced to one-year supervision. Defendant receives one criminal history point for this conviction, pursuant to Guideline § 4A1.1(c).

iii. On or about March 11, 2007, defendant was convicted of misdemeanor disorderly conduct in Cook County, and was sentenced to one year of special conditions. This conviction does not result in the application of any criminal history points, pursuant to Guideline § 4A1.2(c)(1).

iv. On or about December 3, 2008, defendant was convicted of felony burglary in Mount Prospect, Illinois, and sentenced to 30 days imprisonment and 18 months probation. Defendant receives one criminal history point for this conviction, pursuant to Guideline § 4A1.1(c).

v. While under a criminal justice sentence, that is, probation on the December 3, 2008 conviction, defendant committed the instant offense. Defendant receives two criminal history points for committing the instant offense while on probation, pursuant to Guideline § 4A1.l(d).

d. **Anticipated Advisory Sentencing Guidelines Range.** Therefore, based on the facts now known to the government, the anticipated offense level is 21, which, when combined with the anticipated criminal history category of 111, results in an anticipated advisory Sentencing Guidelines range of 46 to 57 months' imprisonment, in addition to any supervised release, fine, and restitution the Court may impose.

e. Defendant and his attorney and the government acknowledge that the above Guideline calculations are preliminary in nature, and are non-binding predictions which neither party is entitled to rely. Defendant understands that further review of the facts or applicable legal principles may lead the government to conclude that different or additional Guideline provisions apply in this case. Defendant understands that the Probation Office will conduct its own investigation and that the Court ultimately determines the facts and law relevant to sentencing, and that the Court's determinations govern the final Guideline calculation. Accordingly, the validity of this Agreement is not contingent upon the probation officer's or the Court's concurrence with the above calculations, and defendant shall not have a right to withdraw his plea on the basis of the Court's rejection of these calculations.

f. Both parties expressly acknowledge that this plea agreement is not governed by Fed.R.Crim.P.11(c)(1)(B), and that errors in applying or interpreting any of the Sentencing Guidelines may be corrected by either party prior to sentencing. The parties may correct these errors either by stipulation or by a statement to the Probation Office or the Court, setting forth the disagreement regarding the applicable provisions of the Guidelines. The validity of this Plea Agreement will not be affected by such corrections, and defendant shall not have a right to withdraw his plea, nor the government the right to vacate this Plea Agreement, on the basis of such corrections.

Agreements Relating to Sentencing

10. The government is free to recommend any sentence within the applicable guidelines range.

11. It is understood by the parties that the sentencing judge is neither a party to nor bound by this Plea Agreement and may impose a sentence up to the maximum penalties as set forth above. Defendant further acknowledges that if the Court does not accept the sentencing recommendation of the parties, defendant will have no right to withdraw his guilty plea.

12. Defendant agrees to pay the special assessment of $100 at the time of sentencing with a cashier's check or money order payable to the Clerk of the U.S. District Court.

Sentence Investigation Report/Post-Sentence Supervision

13. Defendant understands that the United States Attorney's Office in its submission to the Probation Office as part of the Pre-Sentence Report and at sentencing shall fully apprise the District Court and the Probation Office of the

nature, scope and extent of defendant's conduct regarding the charge against him, and related matters. The government will make known all matters in aggravation and mitigation relevant to the issue of sentencing.

14. Defendant agrees to truthfully and completely execute a Financial Statement (with supporting documentation) prior to sentencing, to be provided to and shared among the Court, the Probation Office, and the United States Attorney's Office regarding all details of his financial circumstances, including his recent income tax returns as specified by the probation officer. Defendant understands that providing false or incomplete information, or refusing to provide this information, may be used as a basis for denial of a reduction for acceptance of responsibility pursuant to Guideline §3E1.1 and enhancement of his sentence for obstruction of justice under Guideline §3C1.1, and may be prosecuted as a violation of Title 18, United States Code, Section 1001 or as a contempt of the Court.

15. For the purpose of monitoring defendant's compliance with his obligations to pay a fine during any term of supervised release to which defendant is sentenced, defendant further consents to the disclosure by the IRS to the Probation Office and the United States Attorney's Office of defendant's individual income tax returns (together with extensions, correspondence, and other tax information) filed subsequent to defendant's sentencing, to and including the final year of any period of supervised release to which defendant is sentenced. Defendant also agrees that a certified copy of this Plea Agreement shall be sufficient evidence of defendant's request to the IRS to disclose the returns and return information, as provided for in Title 26, United States Code, Section 6103(b).

Acknowledgements and Waivers Regarding Plea of Guilty

Nature of Plea Agreement

16. This Plea Agreement is entirely voluntary and represents the entire agreement between the United States Attorney and defendant regarding defendant's criminal liability in case 08 CR 1006.

17. This Plea Agreement concerns criminal liability only. Except as expressly set forth in this Agreement, nothing herein shall constitute a limitation, waiver or release by the United States or any of its agencies of any administrative or judicial civil claim, demand or cause of action it may have against defendant or any other person or entity. The obligations of this Agreement are limited to the United States Attorney's Office for the Northern District of Illinois and cannot bind any other federal, state or local prosecuting, administrative or regulatory authorities, except as expressly set forth in this Agreement.

Waiver of Rights

18. Defendant understands that by pleading guilty he surrenders certain rights, including the following:

a. Trial rights. Defendant has the right to persist in a plea of not guilty to the charge against him, and if he does, he would have the right to a public and speedy trial.

> i. The trial could be either a jury trial or a trial by the judge sitting without a jury. Defendant has a right to a jury trial. However, in order that the trial he conducted by the judge sitting without a jury, defendant, the government, and the judge all must agree that the trial be conducted by the judge without a jury.
>
> ii. If the trial is a jury trial, the jury would be composed of twelve citizens from the district, selected at random. Defendant and his attorney would participate in choosing the jury by requesting that the Court remove prospective jurors for cause where actual bias or other disqualification is shown, or by removing prospective jurors without cause by exercising peremptory challenges.
>
> iii. If the trial is a jury trial, the jury would be instructed that defendant is presumed innocent, that the government has the burden of proving defendant guilty beyond a reasonable doubt, and that the jury could not convict him unless, after hearing all the evidence, it was persuaded of his guilt beyond a reasonable doubt. The jury would have to agree unanimously before it could return a verdict of guilty or not guilty.
>
> iv. If the trial is held by the judge without a jury, the judge would find the facts and determine, after hearing all the evidence, whether or not the judge was persuaded that the government had established defendant's guilt beyond a reasonable doubt.
>
> v. At a trial, whether by a jury or a judge, the government would be required to present its witnesses and other evidence against defendant. Defendant would be able to confront those government witnesses and his attorney would be able to cross-examine them.
>
> vi. At a trial, defendant could present witnesses and other evidence in his own behalf. If the witnesses for defendant would not appear voluntarily, he could require their attendance through the subpoena power of the Court. A defendant is not required to present any evidence.
>
> vii. At a trial, defendant would have a privilege against self-incrimination so that he could decline to testify, and no inference of guilt could be drawn from his refusal to testify. If defendant desired to do so, he could testify in his own behalf.

b. Appellate rights. Defendant further understands he is waiving all appellate issues that might have been available if he had exercised his right to trial, and may only appeal the validity of this plea of guilty and the sentence imposed. Defendant understands that any appeal must be filed within 10 days of the entry of the judgment of conviction.

c. Defendant understands that by pleading guilty he is waiving all the rights set forth in the prior paragraphs, with the exception of the appellate rights specifically preserved above. Defendant's attorney has explained those rights to him, and the consequences of his waiver of those rights.

Other Terms

19. Defendant agrees to cooperate with the United States Attorney's Office in collecting any unpaid fine for which defendant is liable, including providing financial statements and supporting records as requested by the United States Attorney's Office.

Conclusion

20. Defendant understands that this Plea Agreement will be filed with the Court, will become a matter of public record and may be disclosed to any person.

21. Defendant understands that his compliance with each part of this Plea Agreement extends throughout the period of his sentence, and failure to abide by any term of the Agreement is a violation of the Agreement. Defendant further understands that in the event he violates this Agreement, the government, at its option, may move to vacate the Agreement, rendering it null and void, and thereafter prosecute defendant not subject to any of the limits set forth in this Agreement, or may move to resentence defendant or require defendant's specific performance of this Agreement. Defendant understands and agrees that in the event that the Court permits defendant to withdraw from this Agreement, or defendant breaches any of its terms and the government elects to void the Agreement and prosecute defendant, any prosecutions that are not time-barred by the applicable statute of limitations on the date of the signing of this Agreement may be commenced against defendant in accordance with this paragraph, notwithstanding the expiration of the statute of limitations between the signing of this Agreement and the commencement of such prosecutions.

22. Should the judge refuse to accept defendant's plea of guilty, this Plea Agreement shall become null and void and neither party will be bound thereto.

23. Defendant and his attorney acknowledge that no threats, promises, or representations have been made, nor agreements reached, other than those set forth in this Plea Agreement to cause defendant to plead guilty.

24. Defendant acknowledges that he has read this Plea Agreement and carefully reviewed each provision with his attorney. Defendant further acknowledges that he understands and voluntarily accepts each and every term and condition of this Agreement.

The agreement was signed by David, his attorney, Pablo deCastro, United States Attorney Patrick Fitzgerald, and Assistant United States Attorney Steven Grimes.

Evaluation

Before he sentenced our son, the judge ordered David to be mentally and psychologically evaluated. That meant he was flown to New York City for a series of mental and competency interviews and a battery of tests.

He called us from his New York holding cell. Kathy communicated the fact in an e-mail to our daughter, May 15, 2009:

> David called today. He is in New York City and says he has a great view of Manhattan (REALLY--not a joke). He said he didn't think he would like a condo there, though. I told him his rent was a lot less than others were paying living there. He sounded well and he says the people, food, and place are all really nice. If you want to write to him, here is his address:
>
> David Schock, Register #40885-424
> MCC NEW YORK
> METROPOLITAN CORRECTIONAL CENTER
> 150 PARK ROW
> NEW YORK, NY 10007
>
> Love, Mom

So David went through the evaluation, cooperated in fact, to what I believe was the limit of his ability. I knew about the report from the court clerk in Judge Norgle's office. But that clerk didn't know whether I'd be able to get the evaluation along with the other public documents. It turned out this was a protected document. To receive it from the court, I'd have to file a motion to have it released. I did file, but did not expect to be successful. When I contacted the court again the clerk suggested that I contact David's attorney, Pablo deCastro. This is part of what I wrote:

Friday, March 10, 2017

> Dear Mr. deCastro:
>
> My son, David H. Schock, was arrested for bank robbery in December of 2008. My understanding is that you worked as his public defender in this case: No. 08 CR 1006, and arranged a plea agreement under Judge Charles Norgle.

I am grateful for your work. You may have thought it odd that his parents did not hire a lawyer on his behalf. My spouse is an attorney (Kathryn M. Neville), and when we adopted our three children, David and his sister and brother, we preached at them long and hard that if you can't do the time don't do the crime. Further, that we would not be hiring lawyers unless there was a grave miscarriage of justice. David admitted his guilt. We urged him to take the plea deal and let him know that a public defender was likely to be the best lawyer anybody could find for his case. In this instance you knew the ground, you knew the court.

[…]

I am trying to make sense of all that has occurred. I have the earlier police records, the court records, the police report surrounding his death, and the post mortem report and photos. The one thing I do not have is the psychiatric evaluation that analyzed David. Before sentencing, Judge Norgle had him flown to New York City for the forensic interview. I think that might convey a lot.

So, at the suggestion of Judge Norgle's clerk I turn to you to ask for a copy.

[…]

Sincerely,

David B. Schock, Ph.D.

Saturday, March 11, 2017

It didn't take him long to respond:

Good Morning, Dr. Schock,

I saw your motion shortly after you filed it. I was saddened to hear of David's passing. I remember him well, and was touched by your request for information. I immediately anticipated the Court's response. I knew right away that the best way for you to get those reports was from me. I started working on it already.

Of course, it is an old file. It was closed and put away in storage sometime before I left my old firm. So I have reached out to the staff at the old office to ask for their help in finding that file. Their system for organizing and storing old files is imperfect to say the least, but I am confident that I will find it.

I'm sorry that I did not respond sooner. I have had back-to-back trials the last two weeks. But I did call the old firm, and I have an appointment to go dig through their storage next week. I will contact you when I have the file.

Monday, June 19, 2017

He had to dig, and it took some time. But his efforts gave me more answers.

Mr. Schock,

I am very sorry that it has taken so long, but I finally got the archive file from my old firm's deep storage.

Attached to this email is a copy of the competency evaluation as you requested. Also attached is a copy of the Presentence Evaluation. This is a report prepared by the probation department in advance of sentencing. It is intended to give the Court an overview of the case and of the defendant's personal history to guide the Court in sentencing decisions. Lastly, I included a copy of the Sentencing Memorandum that I filed in the case to show you what I know about David at the time. In it, you will read that he underwent a previous psychiatric exam while in Cook County custody prior to his arrest in this case. I have searched the archive file, and I did not find a copy of that evaluation. It is possible that I never had it, or that it is in a secondary, or satellite file that is hopelessly lost in storage. I am sorry for that. It may be possible to find that evaluation another way. Let me know if you think it's important, I will try.[17]

For now, you have these records. I sincerely hope they help in some way.

Pablo deCastro

And when I wrote to him to ask if I might use his e-mail here, he responded in the affirmative.

Monday, June 1, 2009

Here is the official report, replete with errors, both those of David's reporting and the psychologists' sloppiness:

> UNITED STATES DEPARTMENT OF JUSTICE
> FEDERAL BUREAU OF PRISONS
> METROPOLITAN CORRECTIONAL CENTER
> NEW YORK, NEW YORK
>
> COMPETENCY TO STAND TRIAL EVALUATION
>
> CRIMINAL NO: 08 CR 1006
> DATE OF REPORT: June 1, 2009

---

[17] And there evidently was no formal report provided by Cook County jail medical services—Cermack Health Services of Cook County—to the Court at David's earlier sentencing on Dec. 3. Federal investigators must have gone to the original files and unearthed the language of David's assessments and treatment. On Sept. 7, 2017, I filled out the FIOA request and forms to receive the records. They came in a timely fashion and contained only handwritten accounts, no formal reports.

NAME: DAVID SCHOCK

REGISTER NO: 40885-424

DATE OF BIRTH: JANUARY 15, 1985

DATES OF EVALUATION: May 6, 13, 18, 2009

IDENTIFICATION AND REASON FOR REFERRAL

Mr. Schock is a 24-year-old, White, male who was admitted to the Metropolitan Correctional Center (MCC), New York, New York, on May 6, 2009. Mr. Schock was admitted to the custody of the Attorney General by the Honorable Charles Norgle, United States District Judge, United States District Court for a psychological assessment to determine the defendant's competency to stand trial, pursuant to Title 18, U.S.C., Section 4241(b). Mr. Schock has been charged with Bank Robbery, in violation of Title 18, U.S.C., Section 2113(a).

EVALUATION PROCEDURES

Mr. Schock was interviewed on several occasions, most recently on May 18, 2009, for a total of approximately five hours. Psychological testing included administration of the Minnesota Multiphasic Personality Inventory-2 (MMPI-2), a self-report, objective measure of personality characteristics, psychological adjustment, and response bias; and the Rey 15-Item Test, a test of malingering memory deficits.

Prior to the interviews and psychological testing, Mr. Schock was informed Dr. Kari M. Schlessinger, Psy.D., Ph.D., is a licensed psychologist appointed by the Court to perform an evaluation. Mr. Schock was informed of the purpose of the evaluation which was to assist the Court with determining his competency to stand trial. Mr. Schock was informed neither the interviews nor the results of psychological testing were confidential, and any information he provided could be reported to the Court in either written format or oral testimony. Mr. Schock was informed he could consult his attorney prior to, or at any time during, the evaluation. When asked to rephrase the above warning in his own words, Mr. Schock stated, "This is not confidential. You are going to write a report and give it to the Judge. I can call my attorney anytime I want. This is to see if I can go to court." It was the impression of the evaluator Mr. Schock had a reasonable understanding and appreciation of the above warning. The interviews and psychological testing proceeded on that basis.

In addition to the interviews and psychological testing with Mr. Schock, collateral phone interviews were conducted with Mr. Pablo deCastro, defense counsel, and with Mr. Steven Grimms, Assistant United States Attorney. The following documents were also reviewed:

1. The Order for The Competency to Stand Trial Evaluation, signed by United States District Judge Charles Norgle, dated February 23, 2009.

2. The Criminal Indictment, signed by United States Magistrate Judge Mason, dated December 18, 2008.

3. The Criminal Complaint, signed by United States Magistrate Judge Mason, dated December 5, 2008.

4. Affidavit from Craig J. Heidenreich, Special Agent with the Federal Bureau of Investigation, signed by United States Magistrate Judge Mason, dated December 5, 2008.

5. Pretrial Services Report, written by Carrie Holberg, dated December 12, 2008.

6. The Share Program discharge summary for Mr. Schock, signed by Amy Cady, dated February 21, 2008.

7. Kankakee County Detention Center psychology notes for Mr. Schock, various providers, dated December 9, 2008 through April 28, 2009.

8. Criminal History Report, dated May 14, 2009.

9. The Federal Bureau of Prisons documents pertaining to the defendant, including SENTRY, Psychology Database System, and BEMR records.

CLINICAL AND SOCIAL HISTORY

Mr. Schock's social history was gathered from his self-report, a review of the above-listed documents, and the collateral phone interviews. Mr. Schock appeared to be a fairly reliable historian and was cooperative throughout the interview process. He often had difficulties recalling dates of events although he could provide accurate descriptions of the events. He appeared eager to complete his evaluation.

Developmental History:

Mr. Schock is a 24-year-old, single, White, male born in Tennessee. Mr. Schock lived with his biological parents, David McNut (sic), deceased, and HiCha McNut (sic). His mother moved out when Mr. Schock was 5-years-old. He was subsequently removed from his father's house when he was 11-years-old and placed in foster care. Mr. Schock indicated he and his sibling were adopted by David Schock, Sr., a movie editor, and Kathy Nevell (sic), a lawyer, when he was 12-years-old, and moved to Michigan. At the age of 16, he left because he wanted to find his birth mother and went to Florida for one year, Mississippi, for one year, and then to Chicago, where he currently resides. Mr. Schock has a biological brother, age 22, who is prison, in Michigan, and a biological sister, age 26, who is a nurse, in California.

Mr. Schock indicated his childhood was "rough." He stated his birth father was an alcoholic who abused him, his mother, and siblings. Mr. Schock stated there were no rules in the house as his father was rarely home. However, Mr. Schock recalled he was often "beat," after his father drank. He indicated his father would hit him with his hand and with objects, often leaving bruises. After his mother left the family, they resided in several shelters, until social services removed him and his siblings from his father's care. While in foster care, Mr. Schock recalled living with several abusive parents. He stated after he was adopted, he was no longer abused. Mr. Schock related since he was not provided with rules prior to his adoption, he did not know how to act and was often "grounded a lot."

In addition to the physical abuse, Mr. Schock received from his father, he recalled a history of sexual abuse. Mr. Schock indicated he was sexually abused by his mother's boyfriend, for a few months, when he was 6-years-old. Although he reported the abuse to his mother, she did not believe him. Mr. Schock stopped visiting his mother, a few months later.

According to Mr. Schock, his birth father is an alcoholic and his birth mother abuses prescription pills. He related his birth mother has been diagnosed with Bipolar Disorder and his sister suffers from anxiety problems. He denied any history of substance use or mental disorders from his adopted family.

Educational History:

Mr. Schock reported he completed the 8th grade. He indicated during the 9th grade, he dropped out of school. Mr. Schock related he obtained his GED two years ago. Mr. Schock stated he repeated the second grade. After he was in foster care, he was given a diagnosis of Attention Deficit Disorder and placed on Wellbutrin, an antidepressant; and Ritalin, a psycho-stimulant. He was placed in Special Education classes. He exhibited behavior problems, such as arguing with the teachers, skipping school, and fighting. He recalled his principal suggested he drop out of school.

Military History:

Mr. Schock does not have any military history.

Employment History:

With regard to employment, Mr. Schock reported he obtained his first summer job, at the age of 17-years-old, as a dishwasher in a diner. He stated he next worked, at the age of 19-years-old, at a grocery store. Mr. Schock indicated he was in a fight, broke his hand, and did not return to work for four months. When he returned to work, he was informed "it's too late." Mr. Schock stated he began working at a temporary agency. He stated he did factory work, however, he would not remain at any place of employment long because he would get fired, when he did not show up. He was not working at the time of his incarceration.

Marital History:

Mr. Schock reported he has never been legally married and does not have any children. He indicated dating "briefly." He stated, "I do not like serious relationships that much." Mr. Schock enjoys listening to music and watching movies in his leisure time.

CRIMINAL HISTORY

Mr. Schock stated he was arrested, for the first time, at the age of 17-years-old, for stealing. He reported after the arrest he was released to his parents. He indicated he has been arrested multiple times for underage drinking, disorderly conduct, property damage, and stealing. He recalled being incarcerated "a few months," after each arrest. He related he is currently incarcerated for Bank Robbery.

A review of his criminal record indicates Mr. Newton (sic) has been arrested for the following crimes:

Arrest Date/Charges/Disposition

December 14, 2008/Property damage/Filed with Court

December 5, 2008/Bank Robbery/Unknown

November 7, 2008/Burglary/Guilty: Restitution; Probation

November 3, 2008/Knowingly Damage Property/Bond Forfeiture

October 4, 2007/Disorderly Conduct/Filed with Court

March 11, 2007/Disorderly Conduct/Filed with Court

March 11, 2007/Resisting a Peace Officer/Guilty: One-year incarceration[18]

July 5, 2006/Knowingly Damage Property/Filed with Court

May 10, 2004/Violation of Liquor Act/Filed with Court

---

[18] This could not have been completely correct. He was, after all, out in October to be arrested again. He may have been in for a short time.

September 17, 2003/Trespassing/Turned over to another agency

November 28, 2003/Municipal Ordinance/Unknown

December 13, 2003/Possession of Liquor/Guilty

SUBSTANCE ABUSE HISTORY

Mr. Schock reported he began using marijuana and alcohol, daily, at the age of 14-years-old. He indicated he would drink alcohol "all day." Mr. Schock recalled, when he was 15-years-old, he used Ecstasy, approximately 20 times, Acid, twice, and Mushrooms, twice. Mr. Schock related, at the age of 19-years-old, he began using Cocaine, weekly. He recalled using marijuana, and cocaine "off and on" until he was arrested, eight months ago. Mr. Schock stated he drank alcohol, daily, until he was arrested.

Mr. Schock attended a 28-day treatment program, the Share Program, when he was 22-years-old. Additionally, he recalled going to Alexian Brothers Hospital, in Illinois, for detoxification, at the age of 23-years-old. According to Mr. Schock, while at the hospital, he was informed he uses illegal substances "to self medicate" and was placed on an antidepressant, antiabuse (sic), and an antipsychotic.

Records from the Share Program indicated Mr. Schock attended detoxification from January 9, 2008, through January 13, 2008. He was then admitted to rehabilitation for continued care. Mr. Schock reported a history of increased tolerance, withdrawal, blackouts, morning alcohol use, and loss of employment due to substance use. In addition to his substance treatment, he was seen by the psychiatrist, given a diagnosis of Adjustment Disorder with Anxious Mood and prescribed Wellbutrin, an antidepressant. He was released from the program on February 9, 2008. His prognosis was "fair."

PSYCHIATRIC HISTORY

Mr. Schock reported his first mental health contact began when he was approximately 11-years-old. When he was placed in foster care, he began attending weekly therapy, due to "acting out." He indicated he was diagnosed with Attention Deficit Hyperactivity Disorder and was prescribed Wellbutrin, an antidepressant, and Ritalin, a psycho-stimulant. Mr. Schock recalled he remained on the psychotropic medication until he was 16-years-old.[19]

According to Mr. Schock, at the age of 22-years-old, while attending a detoxification program, at Alexian Brothers Hospital, he was placed on Seroquel, an antipsychotic and Geodone, an antidepressant, for Bipolar Disorder. He indicated receiving mental health treatment, a few months later, while attending

---

[19] He was on Wellbutrin at the time he left our house, but I do not believe that he'd been on Ritalin for quite some time.

the Share Program. Mr. Schock reported he was placed on an antidepressant and an antipsychotic. He stopped taking the medication when he left treatment.

Mr. Schock indicated, while he was incarcerated, in 2008, he saw a psychologist, at Cook County Jail. He stated he decided to receive treatment because, "I did not know why my life was out of control." He revealed difficulties coping with things without the use of alcohol. Mr. Schock described feeling "anxious, nervous, having knots in my stomach, being really depressed, and overly motivated." Mr. Schock related, "I want to do good, but ultimately I fail. It is a bad cycle." He indicated he was prescribed Zoloft, an antidepressant; Seroquel, an antipsychotic; and Klonopin, an antianxiety medication. Mr. Schock took the medication until he was released from Cook County. According to Mr. Schock, a few days after his release, he was again incarcerated, and returned on the same medication.

Mr. Schock indicated he attempted suicide two times. He related when he was 18-years-old, he was living with his sister and they went to meet his birth mother. Mr. Schock related, "it was not what I expected. I realized my family was a mess and they could not help me." He cut his wrist and as a result he was hospitalized for one week. He related telling the doctors "what they wanted to hear" so he could be released. Mr. Schock indicated he attempted to cut his wrist a second time, one year ago. He recalled being at his mother's house, and again feeling distressed about his family. Mr. Schock related the cut "was not serious" and did not require any medical treatment.

Although records were requested from all treatment facilities, at the time of this report records were only available from The Share Program and Kankakee County Detention Center. The Alexian Brothers Hospital reported Mr. Shock (sic) was not a patient at the facility.

A discharge summary from the Share Program indicated, after Mr. Schock attended detoxification, he was admitted to an inpatient facility from January 13, 2008, to February 9, 2008. During treatment, he complained of "feelings of restlessness, anxiety, difficulty focusing and having a past diagnosis of ADHD." He was seen by the psychiatrist, given a diagnosis of Adjustment Disorder with Anxious Mood and prescribed Wellbutrin, an antidepressant. Records indicated, "he started to become less anxious and began to open up a little more in groups." At the time of discharge his diagnoses were Alcohol Dependence and Adjustment Disorder with Anxious Mood.

Records from Kankakee County Detention Center indicated Mr. Schock first received psychological treatment on December 9, 2008, due to symptoms of depression. He was requesting to be restarted on medication due to recent stressors, such as, "separation, unemployment, incarceration, and childhood physical and sexual abuse." Notes indicate a psychiatric history for prior depressive episodes and suicide attempts. He was prescribed Klonopin, an antianxiety medication; Zoloft, an antidepressant; and Seroquel, an antipsychotic. On December 12, 2008, Mr. Schock's medication was increased, due to increasing anxiety and pacing in his cell. On March 31, 2009, Mr. Schock presented with "panic attacks" and was again prescribed Klonopin. On April 28, 2009, Mr. Schock was seen for a follow up visit. He complained of depression. He remained on Klonopin and Zoloft.

MEDICAL HISTORY

Mr. Schock denied any major medical disorders.

BEHAVIORAL OBSERVATIONS

During his time at the MCC-NY, Mr. Schock resided in a (sic) both typical and special housing units. He was not a management problem and staff reported he was cooperative. He did not receive any disciplinary actions nor was he cited in any incident reports. He was capable of managing his personal care needs. Unit staff indicated Mr. Schock was quiet and interacted well with others.

Medical Evaluation, Studies, and Treatment:

While at MCC-NY, Mr. Lodge (sic) received a routine evaluation, which revealed no significant history of illnesses, accidents, or hospitalizations. During the examination he did not report any medical concerns and was not given any medical diagnosis.

Psychiatric Treatment:

Mr. Schock was seen by the staff psychiatrist, Dr. Diane McLean, on May 29, 2009. During the evaluation, he denied depressed mood and reported mild anxiety. He was diagnosed with Bipolar Disorder, Unspecified, History of ADHD, and History of Alcohol Dependance (sic). He was prescribed Zoloft, an antidepressant; Seroquel, an antipsychotic; and Klonopin, an antianxiety medication.

RESULTS OF PSYCHOLOGICAL ASSESSMENT

Mr. Schock was administered the Minnesota Multiphasic Personality Inventory-2 (MMPI-2), a self-report measure of personality characteristics, psychological adjustment, and response bias. Mr. Schock's responses resulted in a raw score of 4 on the VRIN scale and a raw score of 11 on the TRIN scale, both suggesting consistency in his response style. He obtained a score of T=113 on the F scale and a score of T=120 on the F(b) scale, which places him 2 standard deviations above the mean. Both scales contain items endorsed by less than 10% of the normative sample. Research has demonstrated those who score above T=95 are likely to be malingering or may be exaggerating their symptoms as a "cry for help." As such, Mr. Schock's scores represent more pathology than is seen in 99% of the general population. Such severe pathology would substantially impair his ability to function in even simple tasks, would require a much higher level of institutional supervision than generally provided at MCC, and would be readily apparent to the casual observer. His L scale score of T=43, K scale score of T=30, F-K raw score of 20, and F(p) score of T=106 provide additional evidence of a deliberate attempt to malinger or grossly exaggerate psychopathology. Consequently, the extreme elevations rendered on the clinical scales are not likely to be valid and should not be interpreted.

Mr. Schock was administered the Rey 15-Item Test, a test of malingering memory deficits. Mr. Schock remembered 15 out of 15 items, which does not suggest an attempt to malinger memory deficits.

CURRENT MENTAL STATUS

Mr. Schock is a 24-year-old single, White, male, of average build, with short black hair. He is 5'10"and weight 150 pounds. Mr. Schock arrived at the interviews unescorted, groomed, and dressed adequately in institutional attire. Mr. Schock was cooperative throughout the interview process, responding to all of the questions posed to him.

Mr. Schock mood was euthymic, with a full range of appropriate affect. He stated, "I am alright, not depressed, but I am in jail so I can't be happy." He sat quietly in his chair with no evident psychomotor retardation or agitation. He denied difficulties sleeping or with his appetite.

Mr. Schock denied current suicidal ideation, intent, or plan, and contracted for safety by agreeing to contact the Psychology Department in the event he experiences suicidal thoughts. Mr. Schock was future oriented and did not appear to be an immediate danger to self.

Mr. Schock showed no signs of expressive or receptive speech difficulties. His speech was logical, coherent, and relevant, and he spoke at a normal rate and volume. His thinking appeared organized, and did not appear to be tangential or circumstantial. There was no apparent loosening of associations. No delusions were elicited at this time. Auditory, visual, tactile, and olfactory hallucinations were denied, and none were suspected.

Mr. Schock was fully oriented to time, place, person, and circumstance. He exhibited no trouble with attention and concentration. He recalled all three words which he had been asked to repeat five minutes earlier. Additionally, he was able to count backwards from 100 in increments of one, although he often used his fingers. His intellectual abilities are estimated to be in the low average range based upon his educational history, interactions with the evaluator, and reported vocational history. Mr. Schock's insight and judgment are limited as he lacks insight into his self-defeating patterns of behavior and tends to avoid taking responsibility for his behaviors.

DIAGNOSIS:

AXIS I: 300.00   Anxiety Disorder, Not Otherwise Specified
             303.90   Alcohol Dependence
AXIS II: 301.7   Antisocial Personality Disorder
AXIS III: None

AXIS IV: Current Psychological Stressors: Recent History of Arrest and Incarceration

AXIS V: Global Assessment of Functioning = 65 (mild anxiety and depression)

CLINICAL FORMULATION:

Clinically, Mr. Schock presents with symptoms of Anxiety Disorder Not Otherwise Specified (NOS). According to the *American Psychiatric Association's Diagnostic and Statistical Manual of Mental Disorders (4th edition — Text Revision)*, this disorder includes disorders with prominent anxiety or phobic avoidance that do not meet criteria for any specific Anxiety Disorder-, Adjustment Disorder With Anxiety, or Adjustment Disorder With Mixed Anxiety and Depressed Mood. It includes individuals with significant symptoms of anxiety and depression, but the criteria are not met for either a specific Mood Disorder or a specific Anxiety Disorder. Mr. Schock has a history of nervousness, difficulty concentrating, depressed mood, decreased levels of energy, sleep disturbances, irritability, anxiety, and difficulties coping with his life circumstances. Further, it has been noted in his medical records he has received treatment for anxiety and depressive symptoms. At the current time, Mr. Schock appears to exhibit mildly depressed mood and reports symptoms of anxiety and nervousness.

Mr. Schock presents with Alcohol Dependence. According to the *American Psychiatric Association's Diagnostic and Statistical Manual of Mental Disorders (4th Edition — Text Revision)*, Alcohol Dependence is characterized by a maladaptive pattern of substance use leading to clinically significant impairment or distress, as manifested by one or more of the following within a 12-month period: recurrent substance use resulting in a failure to fulfill major role obligations at work, school, or home, recurrent substance use in situations in which it is physically hazardous, recurrent substance-related legal problems, and continued substance use despite having persistent or recurrent social or interpersonal problems caused or exacerbated by the effects of the substance. Mr. Schock reported a long history of alcohol use, stating he began drinking alcohol at the age of 14. He indicated he was drinking "all day every day." Mr. Schock described symptoms of addiction, including dependency, withdrawal symptoms and receiving detoxification treatment. He reported engaging in illegal activities in an effort to obtain alcohol. Furthermore, his alcohol use resulted in his inability to maintain consistent employment. Mr. Schock's use of alcohol, as well as additional illegal substances, has had a negative impact on his life, as it has exacerbated his mental health difficulties, affected his decisions, and contributed to his criminal activities.

Mr. Schock presents with Antisocial Personality Disorder. According to the *American Psychiatric Association's Diagnostic and Statistical Manual of Mental Disorders (4th Edition—Text Revision)*, individuals with Antisocial Personality Disorder have "a pervasive pattern of disregard for, and violation of, the rights of others that begins in childhood or early adolescence and continues until adulthood." These individuals fail to conform to social norms with respect to lawful behavior, are impulsive and fail to plan ahead, tend to be irritable and aggressive and may get into many physical fights or commit acts of physical assault, have a disregard for the safety of themselves or others, demonstrate consistent irresponsibility, and have a lack of remorse for having stolen, hurt or mistreated another person. Mr. Schock was first arrested, at the age of 17, on charges of Possession of Liquor, Violation of a Municipal Ordinance, and Trespassing. He has been arrested numerous times and reports being "in and out" of incarceration, despite being only 24-years-old. It does not appear he has exhibited any remorse for his arrests. His criminal record suggests he fails to conform his behaviors to the requirements of the law. Moreover, his behaviors demonstrate impulsivity and a disregard for the safety of himself and others. Mr. Schock's aggressive and impulsive behaviors appear to have manifested when he was a child as noted by his difficulties in school, including engaging in fights, skipping school, and arguing with teachers.

PROGNOSIS:

Clinically, Mr. Schock is diagnosed with Anxiety Disorder, Not Otherwise Specified, Alcohol Dependence, and Antisocial Personality Disorder. He has a long history of mental illness, which he often self-medicated with illegal substances. He recognizes his remaining on psychotropic medication reduces his drug and alcohol cravings, while also improving his mood. However, Mr. Schock acknowledged difficulties remaining on psychotropic medication when he is not incarcerated. In light of the chronic and persistent nature of his difficulties, his long-standing substance abuse problem, his failure to seek treatment for his difficulties in the past, and his history of poor judgement (sic), his prognosis is guarded.

CLINICAL OBSERVATIONS RELEVANT TO COMPETENCY TO STAND TRIAL

Regarding Mr. Schock's understanding of the charges and proceedings against him, the following appears noteworthy. He said he was charged with "Bank Robbery." Mr. Schock stated this was a serious charge and he may be looking at 47 to 57 months incarceration. He reported the available pleas as "guilty and not guilty," and gave accurate definitions of each. Mr. Schock described an oath as "to tell the truth." He stated perjury means "to lie." Mr. Schock stated a witness is "someone who saw you do it" and witnesses "tell in court." He defined evidence as "stuff they have against you. It is used to convict you." When a hypothetical murder case was posed to him, Mr. Schock stated "a weapon, witness, finger prints, or a body" could be considered evidence. Mr. Schock said a verdict is "when the Judge tells you if you are guilty or not. It is the outcome or end of the trial." He defined a sentence as "how many years you are given for a crime." He said a plea agreement is "how much they offer if you plead guilty. It is so you do not go to trial and get a certain amount of time."

Regarding the role of the Judge, Mr. Schock stated the Judge is someone who "makes sure everything goes according to the rules." He stated the prosecutor is "the one to try to convict you." He described the defense attorney as "the one to try to defend you. He is on your side." Mr. Schock stated the jury "judges if you are guilty or not, based on evidence." Mr. Schock has an understanding of the adversarial nature of courtroom proceedings.

Regarding Mr. Schock's ability to assist counsel, the following appears noteworthy. Mr. Pablo Decastro (sic), defense counsel, related concerns about Mr. Schock's mental status. Mr. Decastro indicated Mr. Schock had been incarcerated two days prior to his arrest. He indicated Cook County Jail requested a mental health evaluation, while he had been incarcerated. Mr. Decastro reported difficulties when speaking with Mr. Schock, such as he "can't keep information together, his memory is jumbled, and he needs medication." Mr. Steve Grimms, Assistant United States Attorney, reported he has not had any contact with Mr. Schock. He stated, "this is a straight forward (sic) case and his attorney just wants to make sure he is competent." Mr. Schock indicated he has met with his attorney. He related "he is good. I know he is busy." Mr. Schock related he was not on medication the first time he met with his attorney and therefore was "not talking a lot." He indicated the second time he met with Mr. Decastro; it was in jail, he was on his medication, and "I could understand more." Mr. Schock indicated he knows the best thing to do "is tell him the truth and trust he is doing the right thing."

Mr. Schock admitted to having "a mental history, but I still know what is going on." He was recently placed on medication and his mood has stabilized. He understands his need to remain on the medication. Mr. Schock is not currently experiencing any delusions, hallucinations, or other serious psychiatric symptoms which would impair his ability to form a trusting, consultative relationship with his attorney. He is currently capable of maintaining proper courtroom behavior, as well as appropriately attending to and participating in courtroom proceedings. Mr. Schock is fully oriented and in good contact with reality. He is capable of comprehending the seriousness of his case and the recommendations of defense counsel. He is capable of communicating with counsel, weighing the merits of various defenses, and making decisions regarding numerous constitutional protections such as his right to trial, his right to an attorney, his right to enter into a plea, and his right to call witnesses, etc. He is currently capable of testifying in his own defense and speaking during sentencing proceedings should it be necessary.

It is the opinion of this evaluator, Mr. Schock has a rational and factual understanding of the proceedings against him and he is capable of assisting counsel with his defense. It is therefore the opinion of this evaluator Mr. Schock is currently Competent to Stand Trial.

CLINICAL IMPRESSIONS, OPINIONS, AND RECOMMENDATIONS

Mr. Schock is 24-year-old, single, Black (sic), male, who is currently charged with Bank Robbery. He reported residing with an alcoholic father prior to being placed in foster care and subsequently being adopted. Mr. Schock began abusing alcohol at the age of 14. His first arrest was at age 17 and he has been arrested multiple times throughout his early adulthood. He had behavioral problems in school which resulted in his eventually dropping out. He reports experiencing symptoms of anxiety and depression beginning as a young adult. He stated he has had difficulties remaining on the medication when he is not incarcerated. He indicated he was diagnosed with Attention Deficit Hyperactivity Disorder as a child. Mr. Schock presents with Anxiety Disorder, Not Otherwise Specified, Alcohol Dependence, and Antisocial Personality Disorder.

Given the above observations, this evaluator offers the following opinions and recommendations with a reasonable degree of psychological certainty.

1. Regarding the issue of Mental Disease or Defect, it is the opinion of this evaluator Mr. Schock currently does present with a Mental Disease under the law, that being Anxiety Disorder, Not Otherwise Specified. Mr. Schock does not present with a Mental Defect.

2. Regarding the issue of Competency to Stand Trial, it is the opinion of this evaluator Mr. Schock currently does possess a rational and factual understanding of the proceedings against him, does have the capacity to assist legal counsel in his defense, and can rationally make decisions regarding legal strategy. Therefore, it is the opinion of this evaluator Mr. Schock is Competent to Stand Trial.

Prepared by:

Kari M. Schlessinger, Psy.D., Ph.D.
Forensic Psychologist
New York License No: 016617-01

Reviewed by:

Elissa R. Miller, Psy.D.
Chief Psychologist

That report covered a lot. While David was the reporter of fact there were elements that had escaped his memory, indeed if they'd ever been there. In his interview, he reports that he went into foster care at age 11. Heck, by age 11 he'd already been adopted two years.

Most surprising to me was that his father had beat him . . . with objects. Never in all the time the children were with us did that story come out. They had a kind of loyalty to him, I think.

They may well have been right about all the diagnoses. Lord knows, alcoholism and drinking all day, every day will mess you up seriously. But pegging his intellect in the low normal range was a far cry from the son we knew. Still, what did they have to go on but his educational attainments, his work history, and his conversation with the interviewer? Would to God they could have seen and heard the real David, the one I'm convinced was still in there.

And what of David's descriptor first as White, then Black? First listed as Mr. Schock, then Mr. Newton, and, finally, Mr. Lodge? It was clear that the person who wrote up the report was cutting and pasting and doing a poor job of it.

I both wanted this report and dreaded it. In the end I was relieved that David did not see us as a big part of his problems There always is guilt about things done, undone, said, unsaid. I was grateful that he didn't hate us.

David wrote of being back in the Chicago area following his evaluation.

> Dear Mom and Dad
>
> Sorry I haven't written in a while. My sentencing is coming up. and it has consumed me. Once it is over with, I'll be able to put all this behind me, and start my time. Its just there so many what ifs. My laywer says stuff like we could get this amount of time if the Judge goes this way. but be prepared the Judge and the prosecutor could paint me out to be a violent criminal that threatened some body's life in a robbery. My lawer is trying to get me less time, by saying that I suffer from a diminished mental capacity. It was his idea not mine thats why I had to go to New York. I learned that 80-percent of all inmates who go to psch evaluations are caught for lying about having psch problems. Their trying to get less time, but who blames them. Luckiley for me the doctor wrote that it was her expert opinion that I was telling the truth and I suffer from mental illness. But in the end it's all up to the Judge. I have a guide line range, but its such a big gap from the the low end to the high end, plus now the Judges don't have to follow the Guide lines.
>
> Thats whats been going on with me Sorry to be so negitive. I'm gonna keep my head up and take my time like a man. Anyways there nothing I can do about it, it just a little scary. Thats enough about tha.
>
> I talked to Daniel the other day. He seems alright. he says hes having a problem getting a job, which is understenable.[20] Its more than a big red flag when you tell your employer that you been to prison for stealing. Tell him he should look in to programs that are for hiring ex cons. In Chicago there are some programs like that, I don't know about Grand Haven. How is your relationship with him. Mom told me

---

[20] By this time Daniel had been released and was on probation. I think in all he served 16 months, earned a welding certificate, and was firm in his resolve to turn his life around. He lived in a room about a mile away from us. And while we would meet frequently for a meal, he didn't come back into the house. And finding a job was more than difficult.

you only seen him for 30 seconds to give his wallet back. Hope Daniel and you guys make a effort to bond.

I talked to Maggie, she's doing good. I love her, but I have to use everything I got to get trew this bid. I can't be worrying about what shes doing or who shes with. I see people in here tearing their hair out stressing out about their wife or girlfriend. Shes also my best friend so I can call her any time, we share a bond that is more than boyfriend and girlfriend. I got to think about the future, and prepare myself. Shes always been there for me, but this I have to do by myself.

I have been spending a lot of writing what I'm gonna say in court when I get sentenced. As long as it is sincere, thats all I can do. Besides doing that I' have been doing a lot of reading. Write now I'm reading the the 48 laws of power its pretty good. That whats been going on with me.

You son

David
Schock

Wednesday, September 9, 2009

In addition to the evaluation, there came a copy of a memo that had been submitted by David's Lawyer, Pablo deCastro. He had labored hard in the defense of our son. In this memo he is urging for a lesser sentence based on the circumstances. There was no doubt David was guilty, but his capacity had been greatly diminished by his drinking. Yes, he chose to drink. But this is what lawyer deCastro wrote:

DEFENDANT'S SENTENCING POSITION PAPER

NOW COMES Defendant, **DAVID SCHOCK**, and respectfully presents the following information and argument in support of his position for the sentencing hearing scheduled in this matter.

The defendant entered a plea of guilty pursuant to a written plea agreement. The matter is scheduled for a sentencing hearing on September 15, 2009. Defendant has received the presentence investigation report, prepared by United States Probation Officer Kelly Rice. Defendant has reviewed it and discussed it in detail with his attorney. Though the defendant has no objections to the presentence investigation report, he would like to present the following for the court's consideration:

In the presentence report, Part F, entitled, "Factors that may warrant a sentence outside of the advisory guideline range," the officer makes the suggestion that the defendant's personal history and his mental condition may warrant a sentence below the advisory guideline range.

In Guideline 5K2.13, the commission wrote, "A downward departure may be warranted in (sic) (1) the defendant committed the offense while suffering from a significantly reduced mental capacity; and (2) the significantly reduced mental capacity contributed substantially to the commission of the offense." USSG 5K1.13.

Mr. Schock was evaluated by Kari M. Schlesinger, Psy.D., Ph.D., a forensic Psychologist at the MCC, New York. She arrived at the clinical diagnosis that Mr. Schock suffered from Anxiety Disorder, as well as Antisocial Personality Disorder, and Alcohol Dependence. The doctor concluded that these disorders may cause an individual to suffer from, "irritability, anxiety, and difficulties coping with life circumstances." (P. 9). Further, that such individuals "are impulsive and fail to plan ahead, tend to be irritable and aggressive, and . . . may have a disregard for the safety of themselves or others." (P. 9). In addition, his alcohol dependence and abuse has "exacerbated his mental health difficulties, affected his decisions, and contributed to his criminal behavior." (P. 9). The evidence suggests that Mr. Schock's symptoms can be controlled fairly effectively with prescribed medication.

Prior to the date of Mr. Schock's criminal activity, he had been incarcerated at the Cook County Jail for some months facing a burglary charge. He and a co-offender broke into a vehicle and stole a radio. While he was incarcerated, he was evaluated for competency to stand trial. He was prescribed medication, and after some time, achieved a measure of stability. His attorney, an assistant public defender, was aware of his mental diagnosis, and his prescribed treatment. The attorney negotiated a plea in exchange for a recommended sentence of probation. There were no conditions of probation designed to address Mr. Schock's obvious mental health needs. Cook County Adult Probation has a special Mental Health Unit that is equipped to handle individuals such as Mr. Schock. This unit takes charge of the individual prior to his release from custody and puts in place a plan to ensure that he receives the necessary treatment and medication prior to his release.

In this case, the attorney did not request a referral to the Mental Health Unit. As a result, Mr. Schock was released without any medication, and without any plan or contacts through which to acquire any medication or treatment. Within twenty-four hours, he was homeless, extremely intoxicated on alcohol, and made a very impulsive and dangerous decision to rob a bank. He had no plan, no disguise, and no weapon. He did not prepare the note ahead of time, but instead used available paper, a deposit slip. As to his escape, he did not have any vehicle or mode of transport ready. He simply walked away and was apprehended nearby. According to his statement at the time of his arrest, he had gone to his mother's house upon his release from Cook County Jail. She did not let him in, so he went to this nearby bank, initially to use a phone to call a friend. After that attempt failed, he went outside, consumed a large amount of alcohol, and returned to the bank to rob it.

His decision evinces exactly the symptoms predicted by his diagnosis. It was motivated by an inability to cope with a difficult circumstance, exacerbated by alcohol abuse, was extremely impulsive, without any planning, and evinced a disregard for the safety of himself and others. Using the language of Guideline 5K2.13, Mr. Schock's crime clearly occurred while he was suffering from a significantly reduced mental capacity, and the reduced mental capacity clearly contributed to the commission of the offense. His specific symptoms create a danger of exactly the type of behavior that led to the commission of the crime. His actions were impulsive, were driven by an inability to cope with a difficult circumstance, showed a disregard for the safety of himself and others, and exhibited a total lack of advanced planning.

The defendant acknowledges that this is a very serious crime. His behavior put himself and others at risk of harm, and caused severe emotional distress to his victims. He does not seek to excuse himself outright, but he does ask that the court consider his actions within the context of his diminished mental capacity. This Court has the opportunity to avoid the mistake of the Cook County court that sentenced him to probation without addressing his mental deficiencies. Here, his supervised release will be supervised. He clearly needs some time in counseling and therapy in addition to his medication. He simply asks that whatever time the Court orders him to serve, it is sufficient to help him with these goals, but not excessively punitive. 18 U.S.C. 3553 states that the sentence should be, "sufficient, but not greater than necessary . . . ."

He asks the Court to consider all of the information and arguments above. This crime was an outburst caused by a legitimate medical condition. With appropriate treatment, the defendant can avoid such problems in the future, and with the appropriate conditions, can be released reasonably soon without danger to the community.

Respectfully Submitted,

S/Pablo deCastro/September 9, 2009
PABLO DECASTRO, ARDC No. 6224763

In hospitals they have a term for what the courts had done for/to David: "Treat 'em and street 'em." Instead of something that might have been helpful, such as referring him to the Mental Health Unit. I wish they had, but even so, there was no guarantee that David would have responded long term.

I do recall a telephone conversation with him about having been treated at some point and not having access to the medications that had helped him. He was jangling and likely to get worse. And he knew it. In our conversation David had not disclosed how and why he had been treated in the first place. So that arrest and incarceration were unknown to me. I wonder if I had asked the right questions whether I would have received real answers.

There is no surprise that he was primed for impulsive action, especially when combined with alcohol.

Tuesday, September 15, 2009

In addition to the foregoing, the probation arm of the court prepared a presentencing report, something that lays out the crime and makes recommendations for the judge to consider. I call it the calculus of incarceration. The judge—according to a defined formula—ticked off the numbers that established the basis for David's prison time based on the underlying crime (+20), and the facts that the property of a financial institution had been taken (+2), and that a death threat had been made (+2). That made a total of 24 points. From that he subtracted David's admission of guilt and responsibility (-2) and his willingness to assist authorities in their investigation (-1). That left a "Total Offense Level" of 21 points. His criminal history added up to six points, including two for committing the bank robbery while on probation. There was a note that there also was a pending matter:

> The defendant and three others were arrested on November 3, 2008, for criminal damage to property, by officers with the Elk Grove Village, Illinois, Police Department. He was charged in the Circuit Court of Cook County, Illinois, Docket No. 08 MC 3 7385. According to the arrest report and court documentation, the defendants damaged a thermostat in the entrance of a building. A warrant was issued on November 20, 2008, and remains outstanding.

After that, the report reviewed his criminal history and his personal and family history. There are some new revelations as a result of a Cook County interview, things that were not included in the psychological evaluation. Again, there are some things we didn't know:

> The defendant stated that his life had been "so hectic," prior to his adoption, he did not know how to handle a "normal" home. Mr. Schock explained he was behind in school, because he often had not attended school when he was residing with his father, and he felt as if he did not "fit in." He stated his adoptive parents did have him undergo a mental health evaluation, and he was diagnosed with depression and prescribed Wellbutrin. Mr. Schock left home at age 16, returning, to Fort Lauderdale, Florida. The defendant reportedly resided "on the streets" for approximately one year, before he relocated to a boys' home in Mississippi. Mr. Schock explained he had contacted his adoptive parents and they would not allow him to return home, but directed him to the boys' home. The defendant reportedly resided at the boy's home until he was 18 years of age. He stated that his sister, who resided in Los Angeles, California, contacted him when he was 18 years of age and informed him that she had located their biological mother. Mr. Schock traveled to Los Angeles to meet his mother, residing with his sister for a few weeks. He explained that the meeting with his mother was "traumatic" and resulted in his attempted suicide and hospitalization (see Mental and Emotional Health).

> Mr. Schock stated he returned to Fort Lauderdale, Florida, after his release from the hospital in Los Angeles, California, and then relocated to the Chicago, Illinois area, when he was 19 years of age. He stated he was homeless in Florida, and resided with his biological mother, in Chicago, Illinois, for a "short" time, at age 19, but his mother's husband stated he could not care for both the defendant's mother and the defendant, so Mr. Schock moved from the residence.
>
> The defendant explained his parents "want to help us but don't want to deal with the baggage and chaos." Mr. Schock stated he has only seen his adoptive parents once, since leaving home, and does not have regular telephone contact with them.
>
> The defendant's father, David Schock, age unknown, resides in Grand Haven, Michigan, and is employed as a college professor and also edits videos. The defendant's mother, Kathy Nevelle (sic), age unknown, resides with her husband and is an attorney. The defendant's biological mother, Hi Cha Om (sic), resides in Arlington Heights, Illinois, with her husband, and is employed as a waitress. The defendant's brother, Daniel Schock, resides in Grand Haven, Michigan, is single, and was recently released from incarceration for a theft conviction. The defendant's sister, Jun Yi (sic) [----], age 27, resides in [----], California, is married, and is employed as a nursing assistant.
>
> The defendant's father was interviewed by the United States Pretrial Services Office and corroborated that he and his wife adopted the defendant and his siblings in 1998 (sic), and that his son had left home at age 15 (sic) and had been residing "on the streets" in Chicago, Illinois.
>
> Mr. Schock stated he has been in contact with his sister and parents since his detainment for the current offense.

I think David was wrong about us being unwilling to acknowledge the baggage. We knew that came with him; it had to. But he was highly perceptive in his recognition that we did not entertain chaos. And that's what it was. I grew up as a son of a woman who was bipolar. And though I loved her, the chaos that went with that was more than I could take. I have always reacted badly to dealing with those with a like diagnosis. . . .Well, I am not at my best with them. Kathy had her own story of chaos in youth. I know that of the two of us she was better able to deal with it when it came upon us.

David was correct in this, too: we wanted to help him. Lord, we did. We do. But there are times when I wouldn't know what to do that would help—if anything could. There is a certain sense of powerlessness in dealing with someone like David. That's why there's Al Anon. But I had never attended. Would that have helped?

The presentencing report went on to list David's physical health, his substance abuse history, his mental health, his meager employment history.

The report acknowledged that 20 years' incarceration was the top end, but, based on the score of 21 and criminal history (Category III), the guideline range was 46 to 57 months. There would have to be supervised release, and the report called for not more than three years there. Probation would run for a term of not less than one or more than five years.

Finally there were "factors that may warrant a sentence outside of the advisory guidelines":

> Presentation of information in this section does not necessarily constitute a recommendation by the probation officer for a sentence outside of the advisory guideline range.
>
> Pursuant to 18 U.S.C. §3553, the Court shall consider the history and characteristics of the defendant. As detailed in the Personal and Family, Substance Abuse and Mental and Emotional Health sections, the defendant reported a difficult childhood, including abandonment by his mother, abuse by his father, placement in foster homes, running away from his adoptive parents, homelessness, abuse of alcohol and controlled substances, and mental illness. Mr. Schock has been diagnosed with ADHD, Adjustment Disorder with Anxious Mood, Bipolar Disorder, Anxiety Disorder, and Anti-Social Personality Disorder and Depression. Mr. Schock had reportedly been prescribed medication while incarcerated in Cook County, Illinois Jail, but was released without medications and without a place to reside.
>
> In addition to his history, the robbery appears to have been a spontaneous act. The same day he was released from jail, he stated his mother and her husband refused to allow him to reside with them. According to the Arlington Heights, Illinois Police Department arrest report, Mr. Schock broke into his mother's residence and stole money. After he was caught breaking into the residence by his mother, the defendant consumed enough alcohol to be inebriated and then robbed a bank near his mother's apartment complex.
>
> Respectfully submitted,
> Richard L. Tracy
> Chief U.S. Probation Officer
>
> by Kelly A. Rice
> Sr. U.S. Probation Officer
>
> Approved
> Mark Neff
> Supervising U.S. Probation Officer

It was apparent from the efforts of Mr. deCastro and the probation officers who compiled the presentencing report that no one was out for blood. They pretty much saw the situation and David's life in realistic order.

At last he went to court and put himself at the mercy of the court. The judge gave him 34 months, far to the lower end.

There were other stipulations in the sentencing: that he participate in a residential drug-treatment program and a mental-health treatment program. Those two things. And at his release there was a long list of what he needed to do. First, he was to report to his parole office within 72 hours of his release. He was banned from possessing or consuming any controlled substances. No weapons. And he needed to submit a DNA sample. There were other boilerplate provisions.

And there were some special conditions of supervision:

> Random drug tests not to exceed 104 tests per year.
>
> The defendant shalt participate in a drug aftercare treatment program which may include urine testing, at the discretion of the probation officer.
>
> The defendant shall participate in a mental treatment program which may include the use of presumption medications, at the discretion of the U. S. Probation Office until gainfully employed.
>
> The balance of any restitution, upon release, shall be paid in monthly installments equal to at least ten percent of his net monthly income while on supervise release.

He owed $295 in restitution (the difference between what he took and what was recovered) and an additional $100 in fines. The costs of his incarceration and supervision were waived. He could have been on the hook for all of that and a lot more besides.

All of them—Pablo deCastro, as a court-appointed attorney, the probation officers, Judge Norgle, even the arresting officers, FBI Agent Craig Heidenreich—were acting in David's best interests. I will be eternally grateful for that. I think in the end, David was, too, but he could not fully understand what had been done so that he did not stay locked up for nearly the rest of his life (or even all—life in prison can be short).

He went from court back to his cell in Kankakee. And there is precious little that moves quickly in the world of detention and corrections. David wrote about his stasis.

> Dear
>
> How is everything going. I still in Kankakee waiting to go to prison. I probley got at least another month to wait, maybe longer. I talked to Maggie, she says she wants to come visit me. It'd be nice, but I not sure its the best thing. I want her to see me when I'm doing good, not like this.
>
> Could you guys give me JungYi's address I seem to have misplaced it. Also if Daniel has one could you give that too. I'd really like to talk to him. Thank you.

I can't wait to get out. I've got so much motivation to do something good with my life. I know it going to be hard with my criminal record, but thats just going to make me work harder. You can say my life is broken right now, but if I can put the peices back together I can salvage it. I just got to stay humble, and do productive things with my life that move me forward instead of backwards. I always want everything at once, but I have learned that things take time. Believe it or not prison has taught me this. I grown a lot in here. There's no boys in jail, you have be man and carry yourself a certain way. I'm staying positive, and trying to better myself everyday, cause someday I will be out.

I hope bussiness pick up for both of you and I love you guys very much.

Your son

David Schock

David had the good grace to begin nearly each of his letters with the question of how we were doing. At some point in the communication he would express his hope that things were going all right. My work was often uncertain; documentary filmmakers are not in high demand. And by the time of his arrest I had been out of the teaching profession for six years; I was then fully self-employed. In any event, I would usually tell him about whatever project I had taken on. This time I sent him a little fiction piece I had written that was picked up for publication.

Dear Mom and Dad

Thanks for the letter. It was up lifting. I'm glad to hear work is picking up a little. I hope your contract is renewed mom. Im sorry to hear about grandma Stephenson. Is she still living on her own.

Hey Dad I liked the story you wrote. Are the characters in your story real kids you know. I'm thinking about righting a story my self. you know what would be cool, if you wrote a a chapter or a part of a story, sent it to me then I'd add some more to it. Back forth until its done. We could try it as an experiment. It could be fun.

I sorry to hear about Daniel. But you know what he has every reason in the book to be mad, I used to be just like him. But I learned it gets you no where. No matter how mad you get things will never change unless you do something about. Just cause life was messed up doen't mean anybody owes you anything.

Could you please send me some info on these prisons. I get to pick which prison I'd like to go to. I have to go to a FMC (Federal medal center). Some of the prisons, are the same, just have different section like mediums and maxes.

Could you send me into on the just the FMC prisons-
Lexington -- Ky

Carswell -- Tx
Devens -- MA
Rochester -- MN
Butner --NC

It would help so much, cause every prison has different trade schools, recreation. I'd like to go to a place with wieghts. Also I want to get a degree in electrition, or a trade for sure.

I love you guys so much

Your son

David Schock

As David noted, Daniel was having a rough time getting a job. He had been released on parole and was living in a room in a house about four blocks away from our house. I saw him frequently for meals and coffee. Daniel had been lucky . . . there had been other charges in Chicago, and had they wanted to, law enforcement there could have jammed him up with another prison sentence in Illinois. We were correct in our supposition that when he came to Grand Haven from Chicago he had been running from charges. He came out of prison with a GED and welding skills and certificates. But finding a job, a traditional job, was beyond him. Too, the economy was against him and many others. At one point he thought about trying to return to our local Burger King. The manager from his time there was still in charge. So Daniel went to talk with her. She was encouraging and said she'd check with her corporate office. She did. With a felony he was no longer eligible to work there. I don't think he applied to McDonald's.

As for David, he was off to a federal penitentiary, the first of several.

Dear mom and Dad

I'm sorry I haven't written in while. I went tru a little drepprison period. I didn't feel like doing nothing. I don't know why but I've been so down. Sometimes I think what's the point of trying its not going change anything. But I can't think like that. I need to stay positive, and stay busy. When you sit around all day and don't program your self your mind can drive you crazy in here. So I'm doing as much as possible to fill up my days. I'm going to school for majer applanices, and and I signed up for a mecanics class when that ones over. I met a guy on the yard who knows how to play blues really good, and he's giving me lessons.

Hey, Dad I told you about the email, and that it would send you a notice to sign up, but I think I was wrong. You have to go to the corelinks.com and register.

I can't wait to hear from you guys.

Thank you so much for the money you send every month.[21] It means a lot to me. I love you both very much.

You son

David Schock

CorrLinks was a wonderful way to communicate, but it cost, and we used it just "sometimes."

Dear Mom and Dad

How are your holidays going so far. Mine are ok considering the circumstances. I'm in a better facility with only federal inmates. I get to go on the roof for fresh air, and the besement for rec. They got a guitar down there. The best thing thogh is this place has a library. I try loose track of time by reading.

I've been desinated to Victorville Californa. I don't know why their sending me so far. I don't really care where I do my time, I just want to get ot of here. I so tired of being locked up. But who would like being in prison.

Could you give me JungYi's address, and Daniels if you got it. How are they doing have either of you talked to them lately. Did you and Daniel see each other on Thanks Giving. I really don't care about the holidays. Since I left your guys house I been along so many times on holidaays birthdays that I grown to dislike the holiday season. I find them all very commercial, and about material things anyway.

You know not a lot really happens of changes here, so sometimes I don't know what to write about. I know both you stay busy and I'm always interested in what you guys got going on.

I miss you both and hope you guys have a great Christmas.

Love

David Schock

---

[21] We had sent $50 a month to the prison accounts of both boys. We explained this would be for their first incarcerations only citing the maxim that anybody can make a dumb mistake ONCE. Both of them expressed gratitude.

Dear Mom and Dad

How are you guys? I doing fine. I got moved to a cell. Its 21 and 3 which means were out 3 hours and locked in the cell cell 21 hours. We get 2 hours in the morning, sometimes at 8 and sometimes at 10 we alternate between the top teir and the bottom. Im on the bottom and then we get an hour at night, usually after dinner. Its not that bad. I been reading a lot . And I do pushups and situps. I read two books by Anne Rule. Shes a detective writer, but on real people. I read a book she wrote about Ted Bundy. It was interesting. Also disturbing to read what some people are capapel of. Also one about the I-5 killer. Most people I have met in jail are in here for something related to money. But there are some people who are messed up really got no reason behind their madness. I robbed a bank so I'm really not in a place judge others. I find observing other people is interesting especially in place like this.

I been thinking a lot about when I get out. People who know what I did are going to think damn he's crazy, this guy robbed a bank. How am I gonna get a job or apartment if they do background checks. know I can do it though. One important thing I have learned in Jail is patiences. I learning how to control my ADHD and sit still because you have to here. I know one thing I not going to do is abuse my body like I use to. I'm back in shape, and feel better than ever.

I just got this book about the lead singer of a band called The Red Hot Chilli peppers. I dont know if you heard of them. The books called Scar Tissue. The book has fasinated me and inspired me. The guy goes in depth and talks about his feeling he had growing up. The thing that has caught my attention is this guy whent thru the same kinds of childhood I did. One thing that hit me hard was he said he was only a kid living this poor life on welfare and parents were junkies no good people, And he had no clue anything was not normal thats exactly how I felt growing up. I've actually stayed in abandound building with dad while he was getting high and at the time me and my brother would be playing thinking everything was normal imagine that. Well anyways the lead singer ends up becoming a criminal and alcohol and drug abuser. I'm reading some of his stories thinking I did those same exact things. This whole time music was a part of his life, but not on top of his agenda. like in my life, what I not messing up it seems to be the only thing I passinate about. Hey Dad rember when I use to play CDs of my favorite rock banks for you. You always had an open mind. Well this guy ends up over coming being a criminal and a alcohol and drug abuser. And now he is one of biggest bands in the world. Dad go to Youtube.com look up two songs and tell me what you think. You have to listen to the lyrics. Listen to <u>Scar Tissue</u> and <u>under the Bridge</u>, tell me what you think.

You probley already know How but you can listen to any song no matter how rare it is on Youtube. Just type band name/song and it will pop up. You'll get a lot hits so you might have to try a few times to get the one you want. They have a lot of old stuff to like Duke Elington. I Love old music. That what I've been up to Reading and thinking.

Love you both

Your son

David Schock

I listened to both "Under the Bridge" and "Scar Tissue." I could understand how they'd resonate. Powerful music by someone who had been wounded and used his pain and injury to create art.

Kathy had been sending $50 a month right along, but evidently to an outmoded address. He had still received the funds, but it took longer to get to him. So, David set us wise.

Mom This where you send the Money Order, like this

Federal Bureau of Prisons
40885-424
David Schock
P.O. Box 474701
Des Moines, Iowa 50947-0001

the money orer must have my name and register number Just how you did, but I think you have to change the address on the money order. Thank you so much I love you both.

Your son
David
Schock

Dear Mom and Dad

Thank you for the money you sent. It means a lot to me. I used some of the money to buy a radio, so I can watch tv. I try not to watch too much. I workout everyday. I read a lot […]

Hey Dad I've been trying to write songs on the guitar, but I really don't know how. I need some kind of format to follow. I make little riff, but I can't put anything together to make a song. I really like to learn. Maybe theres a book to teach beginners how to write music.

How is your work going? Is bussiness starting to pick back up. I know the conomy is all messed up. I hope this year is better than last.

Love

David Schock

I found a book on beginning composition with an emphasis on the blues and had it sent to him.

Dear Mom and dad

What have you two been up to latley? I hope you guys are doing well. Are you both in good health and good spirits? How is the weather by you? It triple digits over here. JungYi is having her baby soon, that's exciting. How do you feel about being grandparents: JungYi will make a good mom, plus she has a chance to make sure her kid won't have to go through the things we did.

I've been learning some new things on the guitar. This old guy from Philly has been showing me some stuff. He plays blues and funk. I'm egar to learn but he's not a very good teacher. He expects you just to hear something and pick it up right away.

I'm taking a class for a commerical drivers lisance. You can't take the test here, but I will learn everything to know to pass it when I get out. Acually we are going to take the written test but it's not going to mean nothing. I think this would be a good job for me, cause my friends dad is a truck driver and he did prison time. The rest of people he works with looks like they did time too. I trying to be practical of who's' going to hire me and what kind of job I can get, but I still need to be able to make a living. I'm studing hard for the written test and I'm confident that I will be able to pass that. Also my friends dad said he would let me use his truck for the driving test. I hope he still works at the same company cause he was good friends with the owner and had a lot of pull. But I havent talked to him since I got locked up. I trying to stay positive and think about the future. Could you please send me lots of pictures. Some of you guys, Daniel and JungYi. They don't have to be recent, old ones will work.

That would mean a lot to me.

I love you both and miss you.

David Schock

Our daughter did indeed have her daughter, her first child. A short time after the birth we traveled to her home to see for ourselves and celebrate.

David sent us a Portraits of Spring greeting card:

Dear Mom and Dad

How are things going. Things are fine here, same routine everyday. I can't wait to get out. I'm eger to try life again with a new outlook and respect for Rule. Hopefully that will help. I miss you guys so much and love you both.

David Schock

I wrote to him as he neared the end of his incarceration. One of the issues he realized was facing him was unpaid taxes; probably a pittance, but still a fact.

January 4, 2011

Dear David:

Mom has written you already about the tax situation. She is far more expert about that area than I and it sounds as if you might have a fairly lengthy project ahead concerning filing.

We did have ham for Christmas dinner (and the entire week after that). I am not a honey-glazed kind of ham lover, so it was merely smoked, but very, very good. . . . With baked potatoes, broccoli, and pie for dessert. It was tasty and I thought about you as we ate, hoping there was good food on your tray. I am glad there was. More important, I am very glad that you are anticipating your next Christmas outside of prison walls. Oh, golly, it has to be pretty God-awful to be locked up. Your resolve to never return to lock and key again is more than good. I pray with all my heart that you will be able to be successful at that. I believe sobriety is the foundation to make sure it's so.

You have a birthday coming up in short order, again the last while you are locked up. You are turning 27? Wow! I won't say that's old, because it's not, but we have now been part of the same family for 17 years if I've counted correctly. That's well more than half of your life. And with any luck at all you have not yet lived a third of your life. So, where from here? When you start all over again, what would you like to have happen? Yes, a job and a place to live, and the help of the transitional program. I am very grateful that the Salvation Army is going to be there to help you.

Speaking of that organization, this Christmas I organized a series of eight concerts at D&W for the Salvation Army. Lots of great music . . . Dixieland, Jazz, Blues, traditional carols . . . and we were able to raise more than a thousand dollars for the local Sally. Oh, they really need it: lots more people in need and donations have been down.

[. . .]

I hope when you ride out you do so with hope and happiness in your heart, with little bitterness, and with unshakable conviction that your life in the future can be so much better than anything that's gone before.

I send you my love,

Dad

David had been arrested on other matters at the time he was apprehended for bank robbery. There was the possibility that in addition to his federal charges that there might be local charges pending unless the local court system found that his federal incarceration would cover the charges. In an email through Corrlinks, the prison system, date 4/1/2010, subject "RE: First Message," he addresses the matter by asking if we could—if Kathy could—find out what yet might be hanging over his head:

> hey wats up. I got the info on those warents. Could you send me the address to rolling meadows court house, and which department to send it to. that way we can both try. the first one is docket no.08c3307720 and that happened 11/7/2008. the second is 05mc37385 and that happened on 11/3/2008. geting these out of the way would be a big wight off my shoulders. Thanks so much for your help. hope everything is going good. love you both.
>
> David

Kathy reached out to a friend in corrections in Cook County. She supplied the addresses that then were sent to David. Kathy explained the request from David:

> He gave two reasons: (1) he will be eligible for placement in a federal halfway house when he completes his sentence in federal prison (sometime in 2011 I think--we think this accountability would be ideal for him . . .), and (2) he thinks they may let his current sentence for bank robbery apply but only if he initiates contact now. I assume this is the same process my other son went through when he was locked up.

An email through Corrlinks, the prison system, date 8/14/2010, subject "hey":

> Dear mom and dad
>
> I got the money you sent thank you so much. I have some good news. They started my halfway house paper work and the first they do is check for warrants cause you can't get any halfway house with any. Everything came up clear no warrants. Which is a big relief. Now I don't have worry about more prison time. And I will be getting out a little sooner. How much sooner I'm not sure but I should have a new out date in about a month. It won't show up on the computer because your still

considered in prion while you are at the halfway house but it will be a whole lot better than this place. When I get my halfway house date I will tell you guys. When ever that time comes they will put me on a bus and I will have to be at the halfway house in the time fram they give me and I will do the rest of my time there. Thats about all thats new with me what about your two. I love you both.

David

How are you two doing? I am fine. I sent you a letter and I don't rember if I put the right Zip code, so you might not get it. I wrote in my last letter than I'm not useing the Email of phone any more cuase it is to expensive. So please when you have time write me back by letter. I'm still waiting for a halfway house date. I'm getting out soon so, I been thinking about job searching alot. I aplied for my SS card. I sent you a form in last letter that I was a application for a copy of my birth certificate. There was info about you guys I did not know. I hope you guys get it. I'm trying to get everything in advance so I get a job as soon as I get out. I was in the library looking at something, that might help me when I get out and I came cross a thing about apprenticeship programs. It said the Department of labor ensures equality of acces to these programs and gave a web site. I was wondering if you could find out more info on it or give me a address and I could do it. The address is www.doleta.gov/atels bat. Also I found info on a program called Employment and Training Administration. it trains you and places you in a job. It said the type of training and jobs offered veried from city to city. I was wondering if you could give me address to write to the Chicago area one. Cause it only gives a web site which is www.servicellocator.org. I can't wait to get out and try again. Write me back when you have time.

David Schock

Kathy found information on programs, on various halfway houses, on prisoner reentry programs. His first choice was to return to the Chicago area.

He stayed in a halfway house and worked the program. After a few months he was discharged and moved back in with Maggie and her mother. His sobriety did not last.

December 27, 2012

Dear David:

A Merry Christmas and a Happy New Year to both you and Maggie. I was sorry to hear that you have been having serious struggles with alcohol again. That's a hard battle and it's yours and yours alone. We can cheer you on and we can believe that you will be successful—that you have all the abilities you need and the strength within you to succeed—but you are the one doing the hard work of each-day sobriety.

I am glad that you and Maggie have found a minister who can speak to your heart and who can understand your struggles. That helps to be able to say what you really think. And, too, I am so grateful that you are so blessed to have someone like Maggie in your life.

There are no guarantees. None . . . except that we all are born owing a death and until (and beyond) that there is God's love. But terrible things can happen to us and those we love. But sometimes there are wonderful things too that make the living so worthwhile. And sometimes it's the remembrance of the good times that get us through the bad times. It's not always easy to remember that there were good times and you sometimes might have to go hunting for the memories. But it's worth it. Mom sometimes has to remind me of all this; she is a good memory keeper.

Know that I pray for you every day. Both of you. And I pray for Daniel and JungYi and Curtis and Kaylee Lynn. [. . . .]

And from what I understand of your plans it sounds like a halfway or three-quarter way living situation might be a real help to get you on your feet again. As you say, go from step one to step two, not step three, five or nine.

My big project keeps dragging out . . . it was supposed to be done months ago, but writing a book—while it would be nice to have it exactly on a timeline—doesn't always work that way. I hope the book is good; I'm working as hard as I can to make sure everything is right. We are self-publishing it and that adds to the effort. I spend time every day down on my knees about this project, asking for guidance and support.[22]

And then I have to finish a couple of films. They are very interesting projects . . . the first about Native Americans from Michigan who fought in the Civil War.[23] The second is about another poet who has done some amazing things.[24] What I love about my work is that I keep learning stuff if I'll let myself.

I hope you are able to use this little gift to a good purpose. Please give my grateful thanks to Maggie and her mother. They are a blessing in your life.

Dad

---

[22] The book, with coauthor Elizabeth A. Weaver, Chief Justice (retired) of the Michigan Supreme Court, was a damning indictment of the operation of that corrupt court: *Judicial Deceit: Tyranny and Unnecessary Secrecy at the Michigan Supreme Court*. The book runs to 776 pages.
[23] *The Road to Andersonville: Michigan Native American Sharpshooters in the Civil War*, 2013.
[24] *Strong Words: The Art of Toi Derricotte*, 2015.

David did not stay with them long once he started drinking again. And then he was homeless. In a matter of months, he was in and out of alcohol treatment, usually short stints in hospitals. He stayed with friends, on the streets.

In one call I told him about films I was making about contemporary American poets. He, too, was working at becoming a poet. He said it helped with the pain. He never recited his poems to me or sent me any. I did ask.

By June 2013 he was close to the bottom, his hospital stays just days apart, not weeks. He was busted and flat broke, too. So, I sent some money for both of them to Daniel, who at that time had an address.

> June 23, 2013
>
> Dear David and Dan:
>
> I am sending this check on to Dan's address per David's direction. And now that Dan has a checking account, he should be able to cash it without a service fee (Checking cashing places are just another way poor folks get nicked some more.) So, Dan, will you share this with him . . . giving him at least half?
>
> As David said, Dan, you have every right to be proud of your accomplishment: a job, a place to live, even a checking account. Time enough for boxing, for figuring out some things and looking ahead at what you might want to do next.
>
> And right now is really hard for David. No place to live, not enough emotional support, no real outlet for the pain. . . . Except for poetry. Grab at anything that looks positive. I want to encourage you to get to the local library and find some other local poets and go to their meetings. Poetry is serious business and right now it seems like it's the only way to have to speak what is going on with you. And it doesn't matter if the poems are dark. This IS a dark time in your life.
>
> That doesn't mean it's always going to be dark. I have both hope and faith that things can and will be better for you. I know you can be sober, employed, and working toward satisfaction in your life. You have every smart you need to lead a productive life, a life really worth living. In fact, what you are going through now may be viewed as necessary and productive when you come out the other side. There is no telling, and the future is unknowable.
>
> But this I do know: you matter just as you are. You are in this spot and there is a way forward. You matter just as much when you are down as when you feel better. None of this is easy and I'm probably unqualified to speak about the meaning of it all . . . but I want the best for you. Both (all three).
>
> Love,
>
> Dad

David made one last phone call to me, the one where he said he was just so tired of it all; he just wanted to die. It was then I told him I couldn't promise that all would be better, but there was always a chance it could be. Things always change given enough time. It would take that time and some patience, endurance, hope. The only thing I could truly promise him was that if he died, I would miss him like crazy.

Like crazy. I suppose so. I begged him to stay alive.

My own reactions stay in the background, almost as if they were stalking me behind hedges, laying back, sneaking a peek around corners. When they rush in it is as if they have come from nowhere. Grief runs on its own schedule. And this grief is not simple.

Friday, February 3, 2017

I have again delayed opening a package from the Cook County Medical Examiner's Office, this time the paperwork from the postmortem. It is someplace buried on my desk, under all the files of letters to and from both sons, court papers, newspaper reports, school records.

Somehow, it has come to the surface. I thought there would be a CD of records, but no, the package bends. It was mailed January 23, 2017. Inside are the report and the receipt. The receipt, about three-inches square, flutters to the desk and I retrieve it first. The autopsy was $50, and two toxicology reports were $25 each. The stapled report is nine pages.

The case number, 042 July 2013, means there already had been 41 postmortems in July at the medical examiner's office before David's. The autopsy was conducted at 8 a.m. July 4. The Fourth of July in Chicago and the near suburbs is a holiday noted for violence. In 2013, the area homicide total was pushed to about 200 during that weekend. But this wasn't a murder. Still, it was a suspicious death and necessitated a postmortem. In all of 2013, there were 5537 Cook County Medical Examiner cases. Of that number, 2230 would be posted—40.27 percent. There were 507 Medical Examiner cases in July.[25]

David was examined inside and out by Marta A. Helenowski, M.D. I wonder if it was her normal rotation, of if she volunteered for the day's duty, as some physicians do to give their colleagues a holiday? At any rate, this is her report:

EXTERNAL EXAMINATION

> The body is received clothed in navy sweatpants, blue boxers, white T-shirt and one white long-sleeved shirt and white socks.

> The body is that of an adult White male, weighing 171 pounds, measuring 5 feet 9 inches in length, and appearing the stated age of 28 years.

---

[25] Cina, Stephen J, M.D. *Office of the Medical Examiner Cook County, Illinois Annual Report 2013*, https://www.cookcountyil.gov/agency/medical-examiner, 3, 11.

The body is cold to the touch. Rigor mortis is present to an equal extent in all joints. Postmortem lividity is well developed in the posterior dependent portions of the body, over shoulders, neck and face.

The hair is short and brown. The eyes are closed. The irises are brown. The skeleton of the nose is intact. There is a brown goatee present on the chin. The teeth are natural. The neck is without special note.

The chest is symmetrical. The abdomen is without special note.

The external genitalia are normal male and circumcised.

The fingernails are short and clean.

The back and buttocks are unremarkable.

The toenails are short and clean.

TATTOOS:

1. On the left chest, a picture of a lion is inscribed.

2. On the upper back the name "SCHOCK" is inscribed.

EVIDENCE OF MEDICAL TREATMENT

1. On the lower extremities, two EKG leads are present.

2. On the right anterior lower extremity below the knee, intraosseous catheter site with a bandage on top is present.

3. On the left antecubital fossa, a bandage is present.

INTERNAL EXAMINATION:

BODY CAVITIES: The body is entered by a Y-shaped incision. All organs are present in their usual anatomic positions, and present their usual anatomic relationships. No excess fluid is present in the body cavity.

NECK ORGANS: The anterior muscles of the neck reveal no evidence of hemorrhage. The cartilages of the larynx and epiglottis are without a special note. The hyoid bone is intact. [That means that David had not been strangled.] Examination of the tongue reveals no evidence of injury. The thyroid gland displays no abnormalities.

RESPIRATORY SYSTEM: The right lung weighs 982 grams. The left Lung weights 656 grams. The lungs are dark red and congested. No thromboemboli are present in the pulmonary arteries. On cut section, the pulmonary parenchyma shows edema.

CARDIOVASCULAR SYSTEM: The heart weighs 419 grams. The coronary arteries pursue their usual anatomic course, and appear unremarkable. The valves of the heart appear unremarkable. Serial sections of the myocardium reveal no focal areas of pathological change. The aorta appears unremarkable.

HEPATBILIARY SYSTEM: The liver weighs 1974 grams. The liver is red/brown with sharp margins. On cut section, the hepatic parenchyma is red to brown. The gallbladder and biliary tract pursue their usual anatomic course, and display no evidence of pathological change.

HEMOLYMPHATIC SYSTEM: The spleen weighs 218 grams. The spleen is gray and firm. On cut section, the splenic parenchyma is red/brown and congested. No lymphadenopathy is noted.

GASTROINTESTINAL SYSTEM: The esophagus is without a special note. The stomach is empty. The duodenum, small and large intestines are without a special note.

GENITOURINARY SYSTEM: The right kidney weighs 249 grams. The left kidney weighs 266 grams. The kidneys are red/brown with smooth surfaces. On cut section, the renal parenchyma is red to brown. The renal pelvis, ureters and urinary bladder are without a special note.

ENDROCRINE SYSTEM: The pituitary, pancreas and adrenal glands are without a special note.

MUSCULOSKELETAL SYSTEM: The skeleton is intact.

CENTRAL NERVOUS SYSTEM: The scalp displays no lacerations or hematomas. On reflecting the scalp, there is no subgaleal hemorrhage. The skull is intact. On entering the cranial cavity, there is no evidence of hemorrhage. Specifically, there is no subdural or epidural hematoma. The leptomeninges are without a special note. The brain weighs 1339 grams. Serial sections of the brain reveal no focal areas of pathologic change. The arteries at the base of the brain display no abnormalities. Fluid blood is present in the dural sinuses.

SPECIMENS:

> 1. Samples of vitreous, central and peripheral blood, bile, tissue sections of kidneys, liver, and spleen are submitted to the toxicology laboratory for analysis for alcohol, opiate, cocaine, methadone and Xanax.

2. A blood card is placed in the file.

3. Tissue sections are submitted in a stock bottle.

EVIDENCE INVENTORY:

A blood card is placed in a tan envelope and sealed and given to the Arlington Heights Police Department. A written receipt is obtained and placed in a file.

PATHOLOGICAL DIAGNOSIS:

1. Methadone intoxication.

OPINION:

The 28-year-old White male, David H. Schock, died of methadone intoxication.

MANNER OF DEATH: Accident.

Attached were the toxicology reports.

Present in blood and urine were benzodiazepines—drugs used to treat anxiety, panic disorder, seizures, or sleep disorders. They also find use as a muscle relaxant or during alcohol withdrawal. Specifically, there was Nardiazepam (82 ng/mL), Lorazepam (22 ng/mL), Alprazolam (94 ng/mL), and Alpha-Hydroxyalprazolam (5.2 ng/mL).

Also present in blood and urine was Methadone at a concentration of 0.40 mcg/mL.

But he did not die drunk: there was no ethanol in his system. Nor other opiates, nor fentanyl.

Some wonderments: No sign of cirrhosis. And even after years of smoking deeply, no sign of lung damage. In short, if he hadn't been dead, he'd have been really healthy. He could have made old bones.

Dr. Helenowski signed off on the official postmortem October 31st—Halloween—2013. David would have appreciated the timing.

I have read a lot of postmortems in my work telling the stories of unsolved homicides. I thought this one showed care and exactitude.

Thursday, February 23, 2017

I reached out to my favorite forensic pathologist, Dr. Stephen Cohle, of Spectrum Health. Dr. Cohle has appeared in a handful of my films about unsolved homicides. I also have seen him testify during any number of trials. He is always well prepared, and he read the postmortem and replied:

> I have reviewed your son's autopsy report and tox results. I believe that the report is well done and presumably accurate. The level of methadone toxicity (0.40 mcg/ml) is at the lower level of lethal for methadone. The reported range is 400-1800 for lethal.

So, he maybe shouldn't have died at that threshold level. But he did.

Looking over the postmortem yet again—something I still do compulsively—David's post may even have been done quickly, but what's the benefit of loitering? Dr. Helenowski was competent and thorough, both attributes you want in a pathologist. I am grateful to her. My son's body had been in good hands.

And was soon to be reduced to the elements. . . . All after the circus of the viewing of his body.

Of all things to keep, we held onto the metal tag, a kind of dog tag, that the cremator sets on the floor of the oven next to the body. It goes through the fire with the corpse and is cinched in the twist tie at the closure of the plastic bag filled with the cremains. David's tag is deformed and scorched—a sure sign that it's been in high heat, usually someplace between 1,400- and 1,800-degrees Fahrenheit inside the retort.

Kathy scouted gravesites in the city's oldest cemetery. All we needed was one grave; we could put up to six inhumations of cremains in/on it. She identified a couple of spots in an otherwise full section. Two in particular, were within sight of the Civil War monument. A Union soldier, wearing a kepi and overcoat, poised with rifle. I have always held it and the graves of those blessed veterans surrounding it in highest regard. Kathy had a favorite of the two, the high ground near the drive, and I agreed. The site was about 20 feet from the trunk of a massive white oak, its canopy a verdant umbrella in summer and a tracery during winter.

The manager of the cemetery tried to help us get the resident discount when we told her we needed a grave for our son. But, no, we insisted, he was not a resident of Grand Haven at the time of his death. We bought the grave and ordered up a headstone that had his name on it and ours, expecting that we also would have our ashes buried in the same space.

Daniel had been agitating for David's ashes, or some of them. Kathy and I decided simply to inter them, all of them, in one place. And it took a little negotiation with the cemetery staff. I knew from previous ash burials that cemeteries like and expect ashes to be in urns. To avoid last-minute objections I informed the manager that I intended to pour David's cremains from the plastic bag in which they came directly into the hole and mix them with the dirt. Then I wanted to fill in the hole myself, if her crew would leave a shovel . . . and, please, no plastic turf to hide a small pile of earth; let it be what it was. She had to get the okay from the cemetery director. The concern was that sometimes people want to disinter bodies and ashes and move them half a world away. I told her I'd be happy to stipulate in writing that there was to be no further movement of our son's remains. I'd had to file such a letter with the cemetery where my parents are buried.

Thursday, July 18, 2013

The day dawned hot and just cooked through the hours. We'd arranged with the retired priest from the local Episcopal Church to read the liturgy that afternoon. So, at 2 p.m. we met him at the gravesite, the hole tidily cut through the sod and into earth. We brought David's ashes and bottles of cold drinks for the grounds crew that would need to tidy up. I told them that they didn't have to lay back while we were doing the service; they didn't have to stay out of sight. So, they waited close by.

This priest had known us long, had known all three children. One of the things I like most about the liturgy is that it addresses the very somber realities, but is not morbid or maudlin. And there is no homily.

I cannot recall exactly what he read for scripture. I asked him recently, and he said that in cases of tragic death he often would read 1 Corinthians:

> Though I speak with the tongues of men and of angels, and have not charity, I am become as sounding brass, or a tinkling cymbal.
>
> And though I have the gift of prophecy, and understand all mysteries, and all knowledge; and though I have all faith, so that I could remove mountains, and have not charity, I am nothing.
>
> And though I bestow all my goods to feed the poor, and though I give my body to be burned, and have not charity, it profiteth me nothing.
>
> Charity suffereth long, and is kind; charity envieth not; charity vaunteth not itself, is not puffed up,
>
> Doth not behave itself unseemly, seeketh not her own, is not easily provoked, thinketh no evil;
>
> Rejoiceth not in iniquity, but rejoiceth in the truth;
>
> Beareth all things, believeth all things, hopeth all things, endureth all things.
>
> Charity never faileth: but whether there be prophecies, they shall fail; whether there be tongues, they shall cease; whether there be knowledge, it shall vanish away.
>
> For we know in part, and we prophesy in part.
>
> But when that which is perfect is come, then that which is in part shall be done away.

> When I was a child, I spake as a child, I understood as a child, I thought as a child: but when I became a man, I put away childish things.
>
> For now we see through a glass, darkly; but then face to face: now I know in part; but then shall I know even as also I am known.
>
> And now abideth faith, hope, charity, these three; but the greatest of these is charity.

Charity . . . love.

Certainly, there was the burial liturgy and the Lord's Prayer, too.

When it came time to open the plastic bag of ashes, Kathy said she recalled that I had to struggle with the heavy-duty bag that had been heat-sealed. We should have brought scissors. Our friend the Priest shifted in his shorts, perhaps wondering what he'd volunteered for. But at last I was able to tear into the bag and, sweating fiercely, I poured our son's ashes into his grave. I mixed the ashes with the earth using the shovel and then filled in the hole.

At critical times I am prone to think inappropriate thoughts. As I patten down the earth on the grave I was reminded of a joke . . . what a child understood the priest to have said at a cemetery service: "In the name of the Father, the Son, and in the hole he goes!"

Well, David would have laughed.

I don't know if I shed a tear that day by the gravesite. I have cried there often since, but that day the liturgy did what I asked of it: get me through this and let me remember my son in all his possibilities for eternity. The very idea that he would NOT be in heaven never crossed my mind. There is salvation. And it is not up to me to judge who sits at the right hand. And I have faith in a loving God who knows all.

Whatever it was, David's death was not a test of faith. That had already been well determined. But I knew that the sorrowing would go on for years ahead.

Only after the fact did will tell Daniel that we decided it was best for David and for us that he be buried near us, and that we ourselves would be buried with him. All mixed up in the dirt . . . in the hole we goes.

2014

There has been so much that's happened since David's death. My relationship with Daniel spent a time in the "non" category. He called on his next birthday; I hadn't sent him his usual birthday gift. I told him I had no idea where he was living. Well, he was still living with Monique in the apartment above his mother's home. He was going to break it off with Monique. She was abusive, cruel. And he was having trouble getting a job.

At the time of the phone call, I was sitting in the parking lot of a memory care unit in Grand Rapids after seeing a close friend who was suffering from Lewy Body Dementia. My friend would have a couple of years yet to live, but the diagnosis was firm. At the time of Daniel's call I was feeling pretty raw from that and still mighty raw from David's death.

. . . And it hurt, he said, that I wasn't even able to give him a firm hug at David's memorial gathering. In this Daniel was correct. I did not want to grasp him; I was repulsed. But I also knew that I should not have held back. Whatever our distance, it should not have been as wide as the inability to grasp tightly.

With his address I mailed him a check for his birthday, thinking that it bought me some time. What next? How to deal with it?

The "What next?" was foreseeable: Daniel was again arrested. He was arrested for burglary in DuPage County on August 16, 2014, and almost two weeks later for retail theft/disposing of merchandise worth more than $300. He pled and was sentenced to three years on the first count and two on the second, to run concurrently. There was no monthly stipend coming for his commissary account, but I did send the usual Christmas and birthday gifts. I promised him again that for every letter he sent, I'd write back. His thefts had been the result, he said, of Xanax abuse. And that was brought on by grief for his brother. His booking and then prison photos showed a rough young man. He looked too old for his years. The prison booking details indicate that he has two tattoos: one on his chest that reads "Gangster," and a second on his left arm that is listed simply as "Chinese."

He was paroled in early 2016, stayed briefly with Monique and then broke away. They were finished, he said.

And this is where it not only gets better . . . it also gets good. Daniel had met a lovely young woman years earlier. But there was a language barrier; she spoke only Spanish then. He kept her in mind all those years, through prison and then out. And then he went looking for her. He told me that THIS was the kind of woman he had always thought of as the sort he'd want to spend his life with: intelligent, kind, altogether lovely.

Wednesday, March 29, 2017

To my joy, they married in the early spring of 2017. Daniel called me and invited us to come to the Cook County Marriage bureau. Kathy could not come. I hopped a train and got myself there to celebrate this most important landmark. I sensed that he had made a decision to change at a fundamental level. He is making decisions based on right and wrong, owning up to his past, staying out of trouble. I had a chance to meet one of his closest friends, someone who knew David well, too. I think he also was exerting a good influence. Daniel had a regular job in a restaurant then and enjoyed. Then he was laid off. Next, he started working for a succession of plumbing companies; there's been a lot to keep him busy. He shows up on time, takes on the hardest jobs, stays until the work is done. While he has moved from job to job, with each employer he learns something new.

He hopes to get into an apprentice program. He is moving forward to provide for what will be a growing family.[26] I have told him that I am proud of him. I have belief and faith that he can be the best man in the world.

And I am as proud of my daughter as it's possible to be. That doesn't mean that her life isn't without challenges and sorrows. Her biological mother is still an intrusive presence, more so because she moved from Chicago to Los Angeles, too close. And there are other struggles, but those are for her to talk about, not me. She, her husband, and their two children are precious to us.

In one sense, the children have always presented many good possibilities . . . lives they could lead that would bring them joy and great satisfaction. I have been able to see that in them from the first day we met, and I see it still. Despite any struggles, what I see as their truest selves shines through.

That's true even of our dead son.

Friday, July 25, 2014

Some will find this unorthodox, but on occasion I have consulted a seer, Denise King Francisco. She is even recognized by the Roman Catholic Church as one who has the gifts of seeing beyond. Mostly I have consulted with her about murder cases I have been investigating with the goal of finishing a film that might lead to the solution of a crime. I've made six of those films, and so far, police have managed to solve five of the cases, several of them more than 25 years cold. Denise had known that our son had passed. It was my practice when consulting with her to begin with a willingness to hear from those who had a message for me before I began asking specific questions. On this occasion I had not asked about David, but there he was, she said, with a message:

> DKF: First and foremost, your son. This afternoon as I was getting things ready to pour a sweat lodge tonight . . . it was right in here immediately, like right here (indicates her heart). And, um, almost in a beautiful enveloping sense wanting me to tell you how much he loves you. And to thank you for being such a good father, and he was very expressed that I use the word father with you. And, now he's coming in as I bring up all of this. (To David, Jr.) Okay, all right. (To me) Here I am again, he says. This man here is my father. And the way that he's putting it to me, David, is that . . . And he's using the word "poison" in his heart going back to here. And what he's showing me . . . this is very beautiful to me . . . he's showing me somebody bit by a rattlesnake at a very young age, and you were the man who came along who tried to extract the poison that had been placed inside his soul or inside his heart. And he thanks you for that.
>
> DBS: He was a wonderful young man. Every talent. And what Kathy and I saw in him was a great good heart. Poison? We didn't see it.

---

[26] Selena was born December 20, 2017, Liam arrived Dec. 17, 2019.

DKF: It goes way back, and it was his own private . . . private hell, I guess you could say.

DBS: And if we could have extracted that we certainly would have.

DKF: (To David, Jr.) Of course . . . (and then from him to me) I want my father to know how much I love him, and I hear him when he's talking to me, and I hear him when he's thinking of me. Tell him that. Okay? And he's also wanting me to let you know that he has met on the other side the . . . other people you have helped here on the earth plane in balancing the scales in bringing about justice. He says that the work you do even comforts those that are here on this side. He says it's not a one-way gain and that you've put spirits at ease on the other side of the veil with the work that you do. And there's more to come, Dad, there's more to come.

DBS: Mmmm.

She went on to tell me that David was watching, guiding Daniel, especially, but was looking over all of us. He had answers now.

. . . Answers to the questions he'd asked. What would it have been like, he'd wondered in his letters to me, if he'd been born into our family? What would it have been like if his biological parents had been able to raise him in a stable environment? What would it have been like if he had been adopted into the family in Knoxville? Would he have been happy and well? Now he knows.

I do not. And I wonder now if any of those other things had eventuated whether he'd perhaps have been alive.

The Chronicles of Narnia had accompanied David. We wrote back and forth sometimes talking about the characters. Aslan the Great Lion figured chief among them. I wrote to David that of all the things Aslan said to the children. I think the most powerful line was to Lucy in the face of her question: "What might have been?"

"Child," said Aslan, "did I not explain to you once before that no one is ever told what would have happened?"[27]

No one is told. Not him while he was alive, not us. But David loved that book—and all the rest by Lewis. That great lion. It is that image that David had tattooed on his chest. There had been an earlier tattoo there, an identifier of his membership in the Latin Kings, a skull with a crown, something called The Master, a Latin King identifier. But he had added this other tattoo to cover and obscure it. Now, it's also true that Latin king's members use the tattoo of a lion to indicate affiliation, but almost always a lion with a crown. There is no crown here, and besides, why would

---

[27] C.S Lewis, *The Voyage of the Dawn Treader*, (New York, Collier Books, 1970), 136.

David cover over one Latin Kings' tattoo with another? I talked with Daniel about the image, and he said it was part of David's turning away from the gang. Daniel said he was very proud of David for covering up The Master: "Just glad he got that covered up. It says a lot about him, as far as his mental affiliation with his past life and involvement with that lifestyle."

And it's not some highly stylized lion, but a true Aslan, regal, pacific. And over his heart. I knew the minute I saw the tattoo in the postmortem photograph. This was David's message to himself and to me.

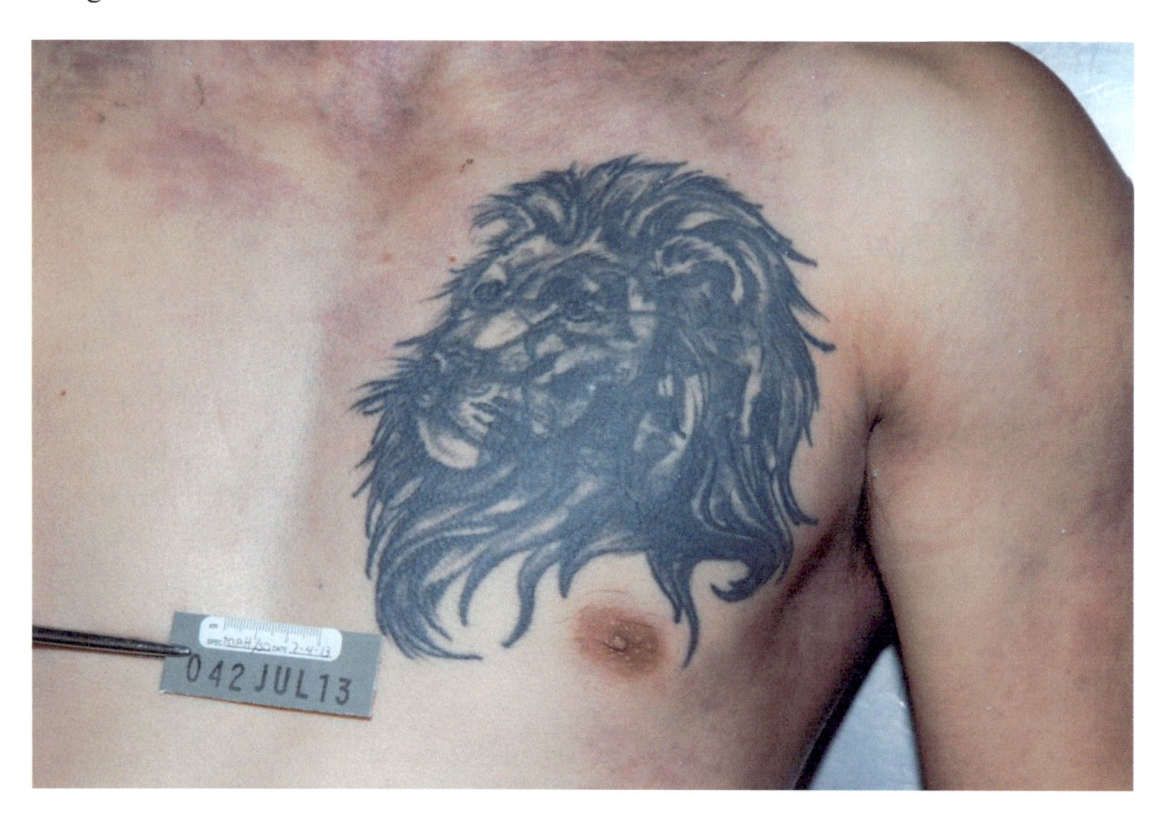

Thursday, July 6, 2017

What have I learned in putting this account together? For one thing, I believe we do not know how to treat people with severe substance abuse issues. I certainly don't. I have wondered if we should have rented David a room, bought all the alcohol he wanted and waited to see whether he'd have come out the other side. Or, would we have contributed to and been complicit in his death? And what about therapeutic uses of LSD? That drug has come in for reconsideration for people with mental health and substance abuse issues. Should we have tried that, no matter how illegal? Where would we have gone to seek such treatment?

And Pablo deCastro puts some of the blame for David's seemingly inexorable slide into depression and death on the institutions charged with justice. This case stands out for what didn't happen that should have in David's arrest immediately prior to his robbing the bank. The day before he walked in to threaten a teller with her death if she didn't cooperate, he was turned loose on probation even though the court's assessment found him unstable. Here's what Mr. deCastro wrote:

> For what it's worth, I believe this sad case shows a glaring failure of the Cook County criminal justice system. He had been evaluated. His attorney and the sentencing judge, were aware of his condition. It was precisely because they recognized how his illness affected his decisions that the Court agreed to give him the lesser sentence of probation. But why not probation with the Mental Health Unit of the Cook County Adult Probation Department? Why not probation with any kind of support? They released him with no support and no resources. His federal arrest came within days. It seems with a more enlightened attitude about criminal sentencing in the first case, the second case could have been avoided altogether.

I am deeply in Mr. deCastro's debt for his advocacy for our son. He certainly did a better job than I knew or understood at the time. And I agree with Mr. deCastro that he should have been sent to the Mental Health Unit. I hope the court has had a chance to reflect on it, and that the next person gets the help s/he so badly needs.

If David had received mental health help, it's certainly possible that he might never have robbed the bank. And if he hadn't done that, would he . . . still be alive? We cannot know. That's part of "no one is told what would have happened."

Thursday, April 13, 2017

There was one other person whom I had neglected to notify . . . Joe Havard, David's boss at the fence-building firm in Lucedale. I hand-wrote a letter and received—probably by return mail—this reply:

> Dear Mr. Schock
>
> We are heart broken and sadden to get the news about David. But we are so glad that you took the time to let us know, we had often wondered about David.
>
> I had my younger son to look him up on Facebook for me some time back and saw some photos of him and maybe a girlfriend. I suppose that he had already passed at that time. We were just thinking that it looked like that he had grown up to be a nice looking young man and all was good. And we were glad to see that. We are so sorry to hear this news.
>
> We have some good memories of David, and the time we spent with him. We all got attached to him while he was with us.
>
> David volunteered to work with me when I went to the boy's home looking for a little help one day. Mr. Fountain at the home said David had been doing good and agreed to let me work him a few days. I remember David being all excited as he

helped me work on a fence project. David always had lots of questions about things, then he would often have a quiet time to think it over. An often came back with more questions or a comment on the subject. Lots of time I would pick his brain on his comments and find them interesting.

Later days passed, David turned 18 and had to leave the home. Mr. Fountain said 18 was the limit for staying. David called me and asked me what he might do.

I decided to let him stay with us for a while and work with me. I just paid him minimum $5.00 per hr. Later we got that little cabin from my neighbor nearby for a small fee and let David stay there. I thought he would feel more like an adult there and not my child. However, we knew he still had a lot of child at heart in him. He was with us (from early Feb. to late July 2003) at Easter time he had a good time with our children, and grandchildren. He went to church with us a lot, I required it of him, not forced, he fell in with my oldest son (a young minster) and looked up to him as a mentor I think. My wife and I have raised 5 children of our own.

Since the beginning of the year 2001 I started a small fence business. After working 40 years in the shipbuilding trade. We have worked with about 31 different young men and women at different times to try and help them get some balance and direction of life. (I hope we have helped)

Drugs are a trouble thing for all ages, but a disaster for the young. God help us. We have always tried to let the ones we work with know about God and the love he gave us. And encourage them to stay away from drugs

I went into great depth with David about God and what God is all about and how he needed God in his life.

David told me one time (as l was picking with him) that he would make sure and contact me some day and let me know how everything was going.

I guess you are his messenger. We are so sorry for your loss, it is our loss also.

God Bless
Our prayers are with you
Thanks for letting us know

We will miss David.

Joe Havard

SUMMER 2017

And I guess I am David's messenger to Joe Havard and others. But if I am the messenger, what is the message?

After all this, the regrets, the loss, the sorrow, there are these things I believe:

First, hope is never false; it may be disappointed, dashed, trammeled, but it endures.

Second, love is greater even than death.

Third, we have been asked many times if knowing what we know now, would we do it all over again: "Would you adopt these three children?" Most often I pause before responding, not because I'm rethinking my answer. I <u>know</u> what I'm going to say. The answer is the same each time:

Yes.

A million times yes.

That's the message.

Made in the USA
Columbia, SC
02 February 2024